WHAT PEOPLE ARE SAYING ABOUT "WHY, GARY, WHY?"

"Your desire to give victims hope, parents knowledge, and outsiders a general understanding.......well, I'd say (in my humble opinion) mission accomplished!

Jody this book will change lives. It'll give hope to countless victims, it'll give countless parents knowledge, and it'll give countless outsiders a general understanding. It's a credit to you that you've had the courage to share your story, and the discipline to finish the book, as I believe that alone is certain to be a major component in the sharing experience.

I sincerely hope with all of my heart that your book is a HUGE success. As such, it will absolutely be one for all of the right reasons. Game changer."

—BENTON ODOM JR.

Classmate and Teammate from Woodlawn High Class of 1990

"This is a book that every parent needs to read. Right now."

—TAMMY KLING

CEO, OnFire Leadership Company

"The Jody Plauché story is a must read for everyone! Jody's resiliency above adversity is empowering."

—MARY ONAMA , LMSW

Executive Director of Victim Services Center of Montgomery County, Inc.

Norristown, PA

"This incredible real-life story of kidnapping, betrayal and murder captured the nation's attention. Now, Jody Plauché captures our hearts with his powerful and compelling personal account of a crime that made history."

—JOANNE GERMINARIO

TV Producer

"Jody does an excellent job explaining human emotions, and in how he tries to help the reader understand what drove his father to take the law into his own hands, while not condoning vigilante justice. He also does a good job of showing that Mr. Gary was a wonderful man who, as a loving parent, was understandably overwhelmed with emotions."

—FRED KIMBLE

Deputy, East Baton Rouge Sheriff's Office, Community Policing Unit

“WHY, GARY, WHY?”

THE JODY PLAUCHÉ STORY

By Jody Plauché

Inspired Forever Book Publishing
Dallas, Texas

"Why, Gary, Why?" The Jody Plauché Story

Inspired Forever Book Publishing™
"Words with Lasting Impact"
Dallas, Texas
(214) 444-6062
https://www.inspiredforeverbooks.com

Printed in the United States of America

Library of Congress Control Number: 2019911501

ISBN-13: 978-1-948903-21-9

Disclaimer: Adult content and adult language. I have tried to recreate events, locales, and conversations from my personal memories, interviews, and a variety of documented resources in order to present these facts in their truest form.

To my mother and Mike Barnett . . .

. . . I'd like to further dedicate this book to all the victims of sexual violence who have not found their voice to speak up and allow themselves to recover and to the parents protecting their children.

ACKNOWLEDGEMENTS

When I started writing this book in the summer of 1993, I set out alone. Just me at a computer at North Lake College in Irving, Texas. I had no idea what I was doing or how to write a book, but I had just received a B in Matilda Saenz's English Composition class, so I felt it was time. I spent my free time in the computer lab (with my floppy disk), jotting down my memories of my childhood. I strung together twenty-seven thousand words of something I thought was important. But when I was done, I did not feel like the final chapters had been written. I felt like there was more to come.

I moved back to Baton Rouge in 1994 and graduated from Louisiana State University in 1997. It was there I met David Hagstad. He was involved in a service fraternity, Pi Gamma Epsilon, that did community service on campus and in the community. He introduced me to Loulou Hong, who was working on her PhD in educational leadership and research while advising an on-campus group known as Men Against Violence. I consider that my start in violence prevention. I joined Men Against Violence and was able to present with Loulou and others at the American College Health Association Conference in Orlando in 1996 and in New Orleans in 1997. So thank you, Loulou and David, for my introduction to violence prevention.

I would also like to thank the following people:

Stephanie Galindo, who took the risk to hire me at Victim Services Center of Montgomery County Inc. I interviewed in New Orleans, Louisiana, and ended up in Norristown, Pennsylvania.

Emily Greytak, who trained me—I learned the most from her.

All my coworkers from Victim Services Center and the board members, including but not limited to Mila Hayes and LaTonya Nicholas, for putting up with sharing an office with me; Kate Hennessy Kelley, for letting me know I was not crazy and writing all my letters I could take credit for; Liz House; Faith Zipper; and Mary Onama—thank you for making my time in Pennsylvania worth it.

The staff and crew at Lone Star Steak House in King of Prussia, Pennsylvania—Mark Riedel, Joseph Daitch, Sean Allard, Monica Taormina Cocci, Laura Contreras Smith, Casie Sauder, Andre Sanders, Adrienne VanderKleut Beyer, Chris Leming, Suzi Patterson-Alessi, and Lisa Worman, just to name a few.

Fred Kimble, Gisele Haralson, and Troy Green. The meeting at Starbucks in 2017 gave a rebirth to this project.

Tammy Kling and Tiarra Tompkins of OnFire Books for helping me complete this project. I enjoyed our many conversations and unfiltered dialogue.

Mason Bettis and David Kenoly. I cannot explain the joy I had editing this book. You two are the best writers I have ever been around, and it was fun seeing you two work. I can't wait for the next one.

Scott Paterno. Thank you and your family for hiring Jim Clemente. *The Clemente Report* is a very important document that is a must read for everybody.

Michelle Morse, my publisher at Inspired Forever Book Publishing. Thank you for putting up with all my changes and edits. Mindi Machart's editing skills were especially beneficial, and the rest of your team made this an easily enjoyable process.

Jim Clemente. Thank you for taking the time to read this book, and thank you for your suggestions. You are the man.

Finally, I would like to thank Scott Berkowitz, founder of the Rape, Abuse & Incest National Network (RAINN). The phone number is 800-656-HOPE (4673). If anyone reads this book and has some type of trigger, the National Sexual Assault Hotline is available thanks to Scott.

TABLE OF CONTENTS

FOREWORD

Two summers ago, I sat in a large meeting room at a corporate retreat in Cheyenne, Wyoming, and listened to Jody address a room filled with hundreds of perfect strangers. He calmly and confidently disclosed the most intimate and disturbing details of his life to a very attentive audience. Being quite familiar with his story, I took time to scan the faces around the room. I noted the reactions of the audience as he spoke. His jokes all got laughs. His recounting of the more distasteful details elicited appropriate expressions of empathy, including a tear or two. It was clear to me and to everyone in that room that he knew how to deliver a speech. I was proud of my friend that day. His speech was very much like the man himself. It was honest, open, a little irreverent, and funny. Then of course, at times, made people incredibly uncomfortable. That is Jody in a nutshell. He won't hide anything from you. And he will *never* lie. (I have a great story that illustrates this. Perhaps Jody will let me tell it at the end of the book.) There are a few instances I can recall when I would have preferred that he lie to me. No such luck.

When he got to the point in his speech when he moved to Texas, I reflected on those days for myself. As I watched him address his audience from behind the podium, I recalled meeting Jody for the first time.

To say that initially, I didn't really care for Jody would be an understatement. The fact is, I didn't like him at all. I thought he was a crass, foulmouthed kid. I had no intention or desire to be friends with him.

One day after psych class, he was behind me as we left the room.

"David, right?" I didn't need to see his face; I had come to despise his unmistakable voice.

I turned and responded with a very flat "Yeah."

I stood there anticipating whatever foolishness was waiting for me. Then he said it. "Has anyone ever told you that you look like Walter Payton?" That was it. Walter Payton was my favorite football player of all time. Anyone who saw a resemblance between Payton and me couldn't be all bad. I concede that's not the greatest foundation on which to build a friendship, but it's worked.

It wasn't long before Jody got around to telling me of his story of abuse. I had recently seen that story on television and immediately called BS. I obviously didn't pay close enough attention to hear the names of the people involved. Within a week of that unpleasant exchange with Jody, I saw the story on another program. This one included a recent interview with this kid I had just met in class and subsequently called a liar. I owed him an apology. I offered. He accepted.

We talked from time to time about him writing a book about his experiences. The more we talked, the more I learned. The more I learned, the more I came to realize that other people could and should benefit from his experience.

When I had children, my messages to them about their bodies and touching and knowing it's okay to tell an adult if anyone crossed their boundaries all came from discussions I had with Jody. I always referred to our talks when confronted with the issue of keeping my children safe. Furthermore, I credit Jody with the level of openness I have with my children. Without knowing Jody, I likely would have defaulted to the Victorian standard set by my parents regarding the subject of sex. Which is to say it was not an easily broached topic in our house. I would tell my friends that my mother thought I was a virgin and that someone just dropped the kids off at my house in the middle of the night. I, in turn, thought she was a virgin also. Certainly, my mother would never do anything as unladylike as have sex with her husband.

Over the years, I've had the honor of watching Jody grow into and embrace his vocation of serving victims of sexual violence and their families. I got to observe his process of clarifying and concretizing his ideas and his message to the millions of people whose lives have been derailed by sexual violence. Finally, I saw him come to recognize and accept the magnitude of his responsibility. As my mother would say, "To whom much is given, much is required." Jody had suffered this horrific abuse. However, he had cultivated and refined this understanding and developed his epiphanic message that needs to be spread. Victims of sexual violence and their families need his unique voice with respect to their recovery and reclaiming control of their lives and their futures. With that realization came the impetus and the resolve to tell the whole story in print.

The story you are about to read will be just like Jody: honest, open, a little irreverent, and funny. When you come to those passages that make you feel like you've been punched in the stomach, just remember that this is a story not just of survival, but of ultimately prevailing against that which seems insurmountable. It's worth every moment. Trust me. Have I ever lied to you?

I have the unique privilege of being able to honestly claim that I am best friends with the most interesting person I have ever met. Jody Plauché is that person for me. In the twenty-six years that I've known him, he has never stopped learning, changing, and growing. It's not always pleasant or comfortable. But I appreciate that also because comfort doesn't facilitate growth. This book is the culmination of that growth and change. I trust you will find it edifying. I hope you will find it inspiring.

Warmest regards,

David Kenoly

INTRODUCTION

"Why, Gary? Gary, why?"

This question was shouted by the police officer. The world watched, transfixed, as this rare type of footage was broadcast over and over to televisions around the world. Upon hearing the officer's question, parents from the farthest reaches of the planet—rich or poor, black or white, Christian, Muslim, or Jewish—could all agree on the answer. I would wager most of the parents watching considered my father's actions heroic and likely thanked him for protecting children.

Prior to the events that led to that riveting television footage, I was just another young American child growing up in a small southern town, trying to survive all the curveballs life throws at us. The vast majority of the world lives this way without the scrutiny that results from television cameras and news reporters broadcasting every painful detail of your life. No, typical lives are not played out on the evening news.

Mine was.

At eleven years old, I was on TV and in the local papers. I was even in *Star* magazine, a national tabloid featuring Michael Jackson on the cover with the story of my experience waiting inside. I felt that everyone who knew me was aware of what had happened to me. Every person in my town would look at me and know that I had been repeatedly sexually abused by an adult man, then kidnapped and finally reunited with my family. The world had come to know me only in that context, as if that summed up my entire story. As if that was not enough trauma and drama for my family, practically the entire globe's television audience was able to witness my father murder the man who had committed those crimes.

During the time that I was kidnapped and missing, my entire life was put on display. When I was returned alive to my family, my mother's greatest fears had been relieved, and her most desperate prayers had been answered. I was not the same person, though. Even on the surface, I had changed, as my hair had been dyed black. My parents asked me what happened, but I said nothing. They found out later from the hospital's rape kit report about the molestation and rape. My father's greatest fear had been confirmed. Imagine trying to tell your parents about that happening to you.

When I decided to write this book, my vision was that you would use my story as a teaching tool to impact your own life as well as generations to come. With this book, I hope to improve your understanding of sexual abuse and dispel myths with truths. I want you to know and rest assured that with the proper support, you—or someone you care about—can overcome most personal tragedies.

In 1992, at North Lake College in Irving, Texas, one of my professors told me, "How you think is how you feel." That simple, resonating statement is applicable: If you think sexual abuse is the worst thing that can happen and that your life is ruined, then you are right. Your life *is* ruined. But if you come to a place of acceptance of what happened to you, face it, and deal with it, then you *can* overcome it and move on. You have this one life to live, and even when a tragedy strikes, you can't let that one thing define you. You cannot allow it to control you and bring the rest of your life down.

I was sexually abused by my karate teacher and later kidnapped. When I was returned to my home, my parents' response was everything. My mother lost it more than once, but never in front of me. Her peace and patience with me were what helped me open up. Through those experiences, I recovered.

The questions I frequently hear are, "How do you function? How are you not crazy?" My perspective is that I had a bad year. I got through it. Now my goal is to teach people that these events are not the end of the world. A bad year does not equal a bad life. It is just a moment or perhaps many moments, but you can get help and get to the other side of those moments and then live a completely normal life (whatever normal is). You cannot let a moment define you. Life is short. If you're going to let a moment consume you, that could prevent you from allowing the healing process to begin.

Believing that you can never recover from a tragedy such as sexual abuse is not a fact but rather could be a matter of misinformation or misguided judgment. Both of these things can be corrected with proper training and counseling. Too many people have suffered under the erroneous belief that victimization defines their lives. Others—such as Robin Quivers from *The Howard Stern Show*, Oprah Winfrey, Madonna, and Olympic gold medalist and professional boxer Sugar Ray Leonard—are the champions in their fields, and they were sexually abused. They moved on. They surpassed the "victim" mentality to become winners in the ring and role models outside of it. They overcame their tragedies and moved on to bigger things.

Many successful people have pushed past the myth that you can never recover from sexual abuse and have become amazing advocates for recovery. Lady Gaga was raped at nineteen, and she refused to become another statistic. In an interview with Howard Stern, Lady Gaga emphasized that her music, her creative outlet, was her therapy. "I went through some horrific things. I'll be damned if somebody's going to say that every creatively intelligent thing that I ever did is all boiled down to one dickhead who did that to me," she said. "I'm going to take responsibility for all my pain looking beautiful. All the things that I've made out of my strife—I did that."

Life is all about resilience. It is my aim to lead people to break the generations-old falsehood that sexual trauma is something that you will never get over. So many different tragedies happen in life. We have the potential to overcome or redefine the way we think about every negative thing that happens to us. After my appearance in 1991 on Geraldo Rivera's talk show, a child from my hometown of Baton Rouge, Louisiana, came forward to disclose that he was being sexually abused by his pastor. He credited my candid story as the reason he came forward. That acknowledgement sparked a realization in me that I could and should use my tragedy to help others. I had witnessed the power of sharing my story.

Ever since I was nineteen years old, I have been following the same plan. Every decision I have made since has furthered my ultimate goal of helping others by speaking out and eliminating that too-commonly held belief that people cannot recover. I have endeavored to give hope to those in distress, because when things appear as though you have struck rock bottom, there must still be hope. There is always hope. Hope that life can get better.

(Please note that even though this personal account is my experience involving a male sexual predator, this is not the exclusive type of sexual predation. I acknowledge the absolute fact that both men and women can be pedophiles, and there are many instances where a female has been the perpetrator.)

CHAPTER 1:

Wake Up

Children are taught not to talk to strangers, but what about coaches and family friends?

The man who kidnapped me was both.

On the thirty-third anniversary of the day of my kidnapping, I awoke to Mom's alarm clock. As irony would have it, it was not a buzzing alarm but rather the sound of a local radio show, which was accompanied by the jarring realization that I had been coaxed from my sleep by the voice of the brother of my kidnapper.

When I think about the day I was taken, the first thing that comes to my mind is the question I am asked the most: "Did you know it was going to happen?"

The answer is yes. I didn't know when he was going to kidnap me, but he told me that he would take me somewhere. Jeff was in debt and owed someone a lot of money, and he had a pending court date. But he didn't have the money to pay what he owed, and he had already conned most of the people he knew in town, so he was running out of options. As the date approached, he told me, "If I don't get the money, I am going to California, and I am taking you." That was it.

Leading to the day of the kidnapping, there were many warning signs, but soon it was too late. I was about to be kidnapped, and yet my parents had no clue. I was teetering between two worlds. A world of youth and a world of identity and adulthood, when most kids take some sort of detour. I was not unhappy to be in a car with my coach that day. But my intuition was flickering a warning light that something wasn't quite right. I just could not pinpoint what was wrong.

That morning, it finally came to me what was happening. I knew he was going to take me, but it never occurred to me to say no or try to escape. I went willingly. Maybe because my parents let me go everywhere with Jeff, and it was the way things were, or maybe because I looked up to him and considered him a friend. My mother had no reason to have suspicions that I wouldn't be coming home. He often dropped me off at home after karate practice. It had become routine. Everyone, including me, trusted Jeff.

When people ask me if the molestation was worse during the time we were on the run, my answer usually surprises them. It was better during the kidnapping because it did not happen as often. When he took me to California, including Disneyland, the number of times he molested me was reduced because he was stressed, and he spent most of his time worried about avoiding being captured. The mounting anxiety and threat of being captured took over his thoughts. He struggled to maintain his act as someone with a calm, loving demeanor.

Today I train parents and community leaders about the truths, dangers, and facts about how adults prey on children. We often give our trust away to someone undeserving. We judge based on behavior and positional leadership instead of taking the time to stop, evaluate, and tread more cautiously.

In public, Jeff acted as though he was concerned about my well-being.

Jeff, being the type of pedophile he was, actually believed he loved me. He wanted to protect what he believed "belonged to him"—in this case, me.

When I was rescued and my kidnapper arrested, there was a moment of relief for everyone, and at that moment, my life changed. It changed because I was rescued, yet it also changed because I was forever thrust into the national spotlight. I was no longer your average, everyday child.

A single moment—a single phone call—permanently altered the course of my family's life. Those events were the catalyst that motivated the media to weave my story into a string of televised events that would cause controversy.

How do you determine if a child has been molested?

So many times, the disclosure of abuse doesn't happen until something conspicuous motivates the victim: catching them in the act, a kidnapping, an STD, a physical illness.

When the police picked me up, they asked me if anything had happened. I refused to tell. I lied and said, "Nothing happened." In my mind, if I told the truth, Jeff would come after me, and I was naturally afraid. I made sure that I didn't say anything until the hospital report came back. Then Jeff couldn't say that I got him in trouble. I would be guilt free and not the person who had ratted him out.

My father, Gary Plauché, was haunted by what had happened to me. When the California rape kit came back positive, confirming his darkest fears, my father went into a deeper depression. The day they brought Jeff back from California, my dad stood at the airport with a gun, intending to make sure he could never harm me or anyone else ever again.

I now understand what my father did and why he did it, but at the time, I was hurt and upset. It was difficult to comprehend because as a child, you learn that killing people is wrong. The emotional manipulation that I had been under for a year had considerable influence over me. At the time, despite all those bad moments, I still felt that Jeff was my friend, and I was sad that he was gone. Years later I realized that I would probably want to do the same thing my dad did if it were to happen to my child, if I had one.

The way my dad was brought up and what he believed was that his first responsibility as a father dictated what he had to do. His dilemma was simple. Everyone knows that killing someone isn't right. When my dad was alive, his only regret was that he had killed a human. Even to my dad, Jeff was a person. That regret was magnified by the hero status that he was given by people who heard the story. They called my dad a vigilante. In an interview, my dad said, "To me, a vigilante is someone who goes looking for it." (Revenge, that is.)

The whole world seemed to celebrate what he did. At the time, I was struggling with it. I didn't want Jeff dead. I thought he was my friend. I just wanted him to stop using me for sex.

One day, maybe a year after the shooting, my dad and I were at the Wallbanger Health Club (now Spectrum Fitness on Perkins Road) when we saw a man who looked strikingly like Jeff. I felt shocked; in that moment, I thought about everything that had happened the year before.

I told my dad, "Wow, I really thought it was him!"

My dad just paused a second and then said plainly, "I knew it wasn't."

Years later, my dad spoke out about shooting Jeff. While he told me he didn't regret it, he didn't recommend other parents follow his lead if somebody has molested their child. My dad believed it was something you could only decide when faced with the situation.

When asked how she felt about what my dad had done, my mom would say, "Are you kidding? Do you know how many kids weren't molested because Jeff is no longer on this earth?"

Despite the tragedy, the ensuing trauma, and the very public spectacle of my story playing out for all to see, I still thrive, and I am still full of hope. I will spend my life being an advocate and an educator about this type of violence, regardless of whether the abuse is aimed at children or adults. I will never be able to comprehend how anyone could be turned on by an unwilling sexual victim.

I feel no shame or guilt about what happened to me. The key to my outlook is that no one ever babied or indulged me. No one ever blamed me. No one ever tried to make me feel guilty. People close to me didn't create drama out of it . . . well, other than my dad shooting my abuser in front of a news camera. They just understood. When seeking to help a victim of any sexual abuse, reach out, listen, and make sure they know you are there for them. Don't rush them through it. Let them grieve and move through their recovery at their own pace. That is the best thing for them, and they will learn that you are part of their recovery. Empower them to facilitate their own recovery, which will give them the confidence they need to become a lifelong survivor and control their destiny rather than being the victim and a footnote in their perpetrator's story.

CHAPTER 2:

Where's Daddy?

As school let out on Friday, March 16, 1984, nothing seemed to make this day different from the rest. My parents had been separated for almost nine months, and I knew it was my father's weekend to have us. As the school bus slowed before my stop, I collected my books. I got off the bus and slowly walked home. I wasn't too excited about going to Dad's.

My grandparents arrived shortly after I got home. They had come to pick us up and take us to our camp at False River, located about thirty miles north of Baton Rouge, Louisiana, in Pointe Coupee Parish. When I say *us*, I mean my thirteen-year-old older brother, Gary Jr. (Bubba); my eight-year-old younger brother, Mikey; my seven-year-old younger sister, Sissy; and me, Jody, just eleven years old at the time.

At this stage in my life, I often found myself pissed off at my father, Leon Gary Plauché Sr. He constantly bitched about not seeing his kids, but when the time came for him to spend time with us, he couldn't come pick us up himself. Instead he sent his poor old parents, Charles Boyce (Gonk) and Annabelle (Belle). It wasn't their responsibility to pick us up; it was his. At least that was what I thought. That was why I was pissed.

We drove forty-five minutes to get out to the camp, arriving at about five thirty that evening. The first thing I did when I got there was walk down to the bank of the river with a flashlight and shine the light on the fish. The fish were lined up, sitting still, like they were asleep. Mikey came over and looked at the fish with me . . . we were about to start our biweekly game of "let's see who can catch a fish with our bare hands."

Every other weekend was my father's weekend to have us. Every other weekend Mikey and I tried to catch fish with our bare hands. To this day, the score is still zero to zero. After about two hours of self-inflicted frustration, I quit. I went inside to take a bath and get ready for bed.

When I was eleven, I usually went to bed around ten thirty at night. I watched the ten o'clock news every night because it made me feel like a grown-up, something I had been feeling for a while. But this night was different.

I was so tired when I took my bath; I drained the water really low and fell asleep. After a good nap, I finally got out of the tub and went to bed without watching the news. I figured missing the news one night was no big deal; nothing interesting was going to happen anyway. Boy, was I ever wrong.

My mother, June Anne Sheridan Plauché, spent the evening over at her sister Honey's house with the rest of her brothers and sisters. They usually played cards, Password, or Trivial Pursuit. On Friday, March 16, they had other plans. They talked about my father, the separation, and the chances of getting a divorce, and they talked about Jeff Doucet.

At about nine thirty that evening, my mother left Honey's and returned home. She planned to watch the news. She knew something she was interested in was coming on, but she never expected what she saw.

My father spent that Friday in emotional turmoil. He went to The Cotton Club, a local restaurant and bar where he often entertained clients and frequently enjoyed an "occasional" beer or two, or three, or four . . . but this day he wasn't in the mood to drink. He called my mother several times to get some information about something that was bugging him. He kept pressing for this information. Finally, my mother told him. The piece of information my dad desperately wanted to know was something I had told my mother. This information had been given with specific details and instructions: "Do *not* tell Daddy."

It was at this point when my dad's plans changed. He knew he had to pick up his children around four o'clock because it was his weekend to have us. He also knew he wasn't going to make it. He called my grandparents and asked them to pick us up because he had something to take care of.

Still unsure of what he was going to do, he left The Cotton Club in a state of confusion. As he drove west on Interstate 10 headed for the new Mississippi River bridge (you have to cross the bridge to get to False River), something came over him. Daddy turned his car toward Ryan Field (Baton Rouge Metropolitan Airport). There was someone arriving he had to see.

Saturday morning, March 17, 1984, my grandparents woke us up early. They put all four of us in the car with no explanation and said we were going back to Baton Rouge. We had all noticed our father had not shown up at the river. We constantly asked, "Where's Daddy?" We got no response but instead the silent treatment. I figured something horrible had happened because of my grandparents' demeanor. Maybe he'd gotten a DWI, or maybe he'd gotten in a wreck and killed somebody or possibly killed himself. I assumed it wasn't as dramatic as him being dead because my grandparents seemed more terrified than upset. I would expect them to be sad if they knew they had lost their son.

We arrived at my grandparents' house around ten o'clock that morning. As instructed, my brothers, sister, and I all went out and played. We were playing on this huge loading ramp for about ten minutes when we saw our mother drive up with my uncle Robert in his police car.

My uncle Robert was a deputy with the sheriff's office (and has since retired). He lived about two blocks over from us in the same neighborhood and has served as honorary "Plauché Disaster Captain." Every time someone in my family was hurt, cut, or needed stitches, we called Uncle Robert. In 1990, when my older brother, Bubba, was in a terrible car accident, Robert received a three o'clock phone call and was over within a minute. He drove my hysterical mother to the hospital and even got in touch with my father, who was out of town and couldn't be reached. At this time, Uncle Robert was always there to help out and never asked anything in return.

Seeing my mother with Uncle Robert, and knowing Robert's role as Plauché Disaster Captain, I knew something serious had happened. At that moment, I thought that my dad had been killed. It was the only logical explanation for why he never made it out to the river. My mother rounded us up, sat us on the steps of my grandparents' house, and told us why our father was nowhere to be found. I had been wrong, and I couldn't believe what she told me.

CHAPTER 3:

My Parents, June and Gary

My mother, June Anne Sheridan, was born in the Bronx, New York, in 1948. Her father was Joseph Morton Sheridan and her mother was Francis Rodriguez Sheridan (Maw-Maw). Prior to my mother's birth, Joseph and Francis had two children. Honey was their oldest daughter, and Dinah was the second daughter. Then came June, another daughter. They left New York in 1950 when June was around two years old and moved to Baton Rouge, Louisiana.

Joseph and Francis went on to have three more children: Robert, Michael, and Patty. My mother described her father, Joseph, as very strict, very stern, and also very educated. June loved her father but resents the fact that he only said "I love you" one time. She was seventeen. Her father, Joseph was sick, very sick. He knew, in fact, that he was dying. The very next day, February 19, 1966, he died of amyloidosis. Amyloidosis is a rare disease that occurs when a substance called an amyloid builds up in your organs. An amyloid is an abnormal protein that is produced in your bone marrow and can be deposited in any tissue or organ. In 1966, Joseph was one of the handful of people in America who had been known to have died of this rare disease.

For most of my mother's childhood, they lived in a small house on Government Street. Joseph took a job as a photographer, and Francis stayed home to raise six children. The children attended Our Lady of Mercy, a private Catholic school with a reputation for strict rules and harsh discipline.

My mother spent most of her time at Cynthia and Guy Dicharry's house. She would babysit Cynthia and Guy's four children: Guy Jr., Dickie, Stevie, and Lilly Ann. My mother admired Cynthia because her house was the neighborhood hangout. All the kids in the neighborhood were welcome. She felt her household, on the other hand, was not as receptive. That was because of her father and his grim personality.

My mother always said, "When I grow up, I want to be just like Cynthia." Ironically, my mother had three boys and a youngest girl, just like Cynthia. Her house was open to the neighborhood kids, just like Cynthia's. She felt lucky that her life mirrored that of the woman she so admired. Her wish had indeed come true. The similarities were so prevalent that she feared how far they would go. In fact, on the day before my eighteenth birthday, I was not allowed to leave the house. That's because Dickie, Cynthia's second son, was killed in a car accident one day before his eighteenth birthday (at least that's what my mother thought). Only *after* I wasn't allowed to do anything that day, Steven, Cynthia's third son, reminded my mother that Dickie had died the day before his *nineteenth* birthday.

When my mother was fifteen, her family moved to Taos, New Mexico. She lived in Taos for three years, until her father died. She made many friends and still feels connected to Taos. To this day her face lights up with joy when she speaks of Taos. In September of 2017, she and I were able to make a trip there to visit her old friends and reminisce on her high school memories for her fiftieth class reunion.

My father, Leon Gary Plauché, was born on November 10, 1945, at Our Lady of the Lake Regional Medical Center in Baton Rouge, Louisiana. His father was Charles Boyce Plauché, and his mother was Annabelle Jefferies Plauché. Charles worked for Standard Oil, and Belle . . . she just had her hands full taking care of Gary and his older brother, Jeffrey Lynn. Gary wasn't a problem child, but he always stayed in trouble (so I guess he *was* a problem child). One teacher in elementary school told my father she would give him an A if he just behaved himself. He got a C.

Another time, when members of the school board visited his high school, he did his best to make sure the school would look good. Just as all the administrators were approaching, he filled a condom with water at the nearest water fountain. I'm sure that made a good impression.

Gary was, however, an all-star sprinter in track, so I was told. He said that at the time, he held the fastest state time in the fifty-yard dash. (Yes, the fifty-yard dash used to be a thing.) He said he wasn't as good in the hundred-yard dash because that was when the cigarette lungs kicked in.

But regardless of all the mischief my father caused, his greatest asset seemed to get him out of trouble—that being his personality. He knew everybody, and everybody loved him. Despite his hyperactive ways, my father was softhearted and kind, generous and helpful. There wasn't a stray animal he didn't pick up and feed, and he couldn't go anywhere without running into somebody he knew.

When I was young, he used to take me and my brother to Louisiana State University (LSU) football games, and it would take us forty-five minutes to an hour just to get to our seats because he would stop and talk to every person seated in the same section and two to three sections over. It was frustrating at the time, but I grew to be amazed by the number of people who knew and loved my dad.

When my mother moved back to Baton Rouge, she got a job singing at a local nightclub. This was where they met. June was intrigued by Gary's personality and sense of humor. Gary, in a sense, swept June off her feet. They began an extremely short courtship lasting only a month. On December 25, 1969, my parents were married.

Because they were married so quickly and weren't even really engaged, I asked my mom why she got married so quickly. She said, "Your dad made me laugh. He made me happy."

Their first year of marriage was like a dream to June and Gary. In October 1970, June gave birth to Gary Jr. (Bubba). They lived in Biloxi, Mississippi, where Gary served as a medic in the US Air Force. They rented a house from Jack Graham and often visited their good friends Raymond and Lois Egers. (Later, Raymond and Lois would become my godparents).

But shortly after Bubba was born, June realized something she hadn't noticed before. Gary was drinking more and more. He began to stay out later and later with his friends, while June was left at home to take care of an infant by herself. Eventually, this man who had once made her laugh and be happy was never around. When he was around, he was drunk, and this took a toll on June and her happiness.

Inevitably, June was unable to take much more of Gary's drinking. June began to consider ways to leave him. There was one thing concerning June that she had to check out. And when she walked out of the doctor's office, it had been confirmed—she was pregnant again . . . with me. That was when she realized there was no way she could leave. She could barely support one baby, much less two.

In May of 1971, Gary and June moved back to Baton Rouge. That fall, they planned to go see LSU and Notre Dame play football in Tiger Stadium, also known as Death Valley, on a Saturday night. Unexpectedly, June experienced complications with her pregnancy, and under doctor's orders, she stayed home and missed the game she had really wanted to attend. I had not even been born yet, and this was the second time I had caused problems for my mother. She should have known right then that I had things in store for her.

On April 27, 1972, at 2:41 p.m., I, Joseph Boyce Plauché, was born. This didn't change much in June and Gary's relationship. Gary got a job working for Baton Rouge Wholesale Liquor. This was probably the worst place he could have gotten a job. Almost every day, he would come home from work drunk. This left June to take care of two kids and one grown man.

My dad would spend his workday drinking, eating out, and bullshitting with his friends, which wasn't that bad because he met and befriended more people than you can imagine. Each person he met, he charmed with his wit and compelled with his personality. Everyone loved my dad. Women and men alike felt my mother was lucky to be married to such a wonderful man. But my mother felt differently.

She came to resent his popularity and standing in the community. I think what she really resented was the fact that everyone who thought he was so wonderful got to spend time with him but her. My mother and my father did not spend any quality time together. The time they did spend together, Daddy was drunk. Other times, Daddy would entertain their friends while my mother served as hostess, waitress, prep cook, and cleanup crew.

After two boys, my mother was ready to try for a girl. She got pregnant with their third child, whom they eventually named Jeffrey Michael (Mikey). She'd wanted a girl but got a boy. A year after Mikey was born, my mother got some news she was not particularly pleased to hear—she was pregnant *again.* I remember the day she found out. We were at my aunt Patty's house in Denham Springs, Louisiana, and my mom was crying hysterically. The grown-ups told us she was so happy she was crying. But I knew different. I knew she was not happy. She went on to cry for a solid week.

On March 9, 1977, June had the baby girl she'd always wanted. At last, she had three boys and a youngest girl, just like Cynthia. The baby girl was named Jennifer Laureé Plauché, but everyone called her Sissy. Later, Mom paid to have Sissy included in her legal name.

My parents' relationship continued to fizzle. But Mom, like a lot of other women, felt trapped with four kids and merely a high school education. I don't recall my parents ever showing any kind of affection for one another. Finally, in the summer of 1983, eleven years after she'd first decided to leave, my mother asked my father to leave. She'd had enough.

CHAPTER 4:

My Family

My brother Bubba is the oldest of Mom and Dad's four children. He was born October 3, 1970, at Keesler Air Force Base in Biloxi, Mississippi. From the time he was old enough to stand, he had a football or a baseball in his hands. He was a year old when the family moved back to Baton Rouge.

Since Bubba was only eighteen months older than me, he was always there for me to play with. Growing up, he was my best friend. We always played on the same sports teams, and when we were young, my mother dressed us alike. People often thought we were twins.

Bubba's first love may have been football, but he excelled in baseball at Woodlawn High. In high school, he was an all-district center fielder. In football, though, the sport he loved so much, he never had a chance to show he could play. He was a receiver. However, the coach was reluctant to play him because did not possess receiver speed. Finally, with four games left in his senior year, he got a chance to show what he could do. He could catch. He caught five passes in the next-to-last game of the year. At the time, it was a school record, I believe. That doesn't sound like much, but our football team wasn't known for its aerial attack.

In the fall of 1990, after an unsuccessful academic attempt at LSU, Bubba moved away from home. He moved in with our uncle Jeff in Irving, Texas, where he attended North Lake College. At North Lake, his grades improved, and he made the baseball team. When he came to visit over Christmas break, it was easy to see that Bubba had been working out and getting in shape. He looked good.

On December 15, 1990, he was in a terrible car accident. He was the passenger in a one-car drunk-driver accident, and the jeep they were in ran off the road and into a railroad light. The jeep then flipped several times. Bubba was fastened in but still suffered major injuries. He broke every bone in his face along with bones in his shoulder and neck. He did not know that the driver of the jeep was intoxicated.

He was in intensive care for a week and was put on a breathing machine. He underwent six hours and forty-five minutes of reconstructive plastic surgery. Today, he still has weakened vision in one eye, his shoulder still bothers him, and he sets off the metal detectors in airports because of all the plates and screws in his head.

Mikey, my younger brother, was born July 31, 1975. He was, and still is, hyperactive. That is a trait passed down from our father. His energetic persona made it a challenge to keep him from getting into things and getting in trouble. After I was born, my mother thought there could never be a kid who was as difficult as I was. She was wrong; Mikey was even more of a challenge than I was.

Mikey also suffers from severe learning disabilities and dyslexia. He struggled through school and was held back twice. Mikey wasn't blessed with athletic abilities or interest like me and Bubba. Mikey was too spastic and uncoordinated. But during his tenth-grade year, he finally found a sport he was interested in and good at: pole vaulting.

Pole vaulting requires the same reckless mentality with which Mikey lives life and drives a car. You have to be adventurous and daring. Mikey was the district pole vault champion in 1993, though he had no recognizable form or technique. At times, he looked like a dancer in the air. Other times, he looked more like a Taser victim in the air—cussing, yelling, and spitting. Anything to clear the bar.

Sissy, the only girl and the youngest of four children, is the "princess" of the family. She was always pampered and babied. Sissy always got her way because she was the youngest and a girl. My grandmother spoiled her with more clothes than a human can wear in a lifetime. She was always getting new suits and outfits, while we got a patch to cover the holes in our jeans. (That is a bit exaggerated, but back then, that is exactly how it seemed). Growing up with three older brothers, Sissy was tougher than most girls. She didn't let anyone walk all over her, and it would be inadvisable to engage her in a fight. She literally fights like a man. Once at Calloway's, a Baton Rouge health club, Stormy Daniels, who became famous in 2018 when the public learned of her alleged affair with President Donald Trump, threw a smoothie in my sister's face. What happened next would likely put a smile on every Trump supporter's face. My sister whupped her ass. In Sissy's words, "Not as bad as I wanted to . . . but I got her pretty good." But now, Stormy is a great follow on Twitter and is hilarious. I enjoyed reading her book because of the references to Baton Rouge.

To illustrate how small of a town Baton Rouge was back then and, in a way, still is, Donnie Calloway bought the health club that was originally opened by Guy Bellelo. Guy Bellelo was good friends with my father and paid for his defense later. Sissy now has a daughter with Donnie Calloway's brother, Kevin. Sissy met Kevin while bartending at a bar across the street from Calloway's health club. At the health club, Sissy fought the porn star who allegedly screwed the president. The health club was also across the street from the karate school where Jeff started to molest me, which was next door to the bar where Sissy met Kevin. That's some "sands through the hourglass" shit right there.

Our favorite thing to do to mess with Sissy was to beat the shit out of her baby dolls. Bubba and I would pretend we were the Junkyard Dog and Cocoa Samoa (professional wrestlers) and "come off the top rope" on Raggedy Ann and Raggedy Andy while Sissy pitched a screaming, crying fit. She would tell on us, and we would have to quit. But we always got one last dropkick in as we left the room.

Sissy has always been pretty. When she was in high school, she did not look like she was in high school. She looked older. While she was visiting me in Dallas, guys always stared as we entered the room together, only to be amazed to learn she was only fourteen. They wouldn't believe it. Some even asked to see her driver's license. But she was only fourteen and didn't have one.

When Bubba and I were growing up, he was the shy one, and I was the outgoing one. When Mom said we couldn't do something, I was the one to go fight for the cause, and I still am. Needless to say, I got slapped and punished more often than Bubba did. With girls, it was the same way. I would go talk to them, get their number, and call them. Of course, they would then get my number and call back asking for Bubba.

I was the one who told my mother everything because I could never keep my mouth shut, even when I knew I should. Once when I was five, I was out at Bubba's football practice (my dad was the coach), and I wandered over to where the older boys were practicing on the field next to me. Bryan Blake, a friend and neighbor, was sitting with a few of his friends under a tree. Naturally, seeing Bryan, I wanted to talk with him. Well, I did talk with him and his friends, but one of his friends filled me in on some subjects I didn't quite understand. At the time, I was worried because they told me "dirty" stuff. I knew I would get in trouble if my mother found out I'd heard this. Of course, I went home and told on myself. My mother stood there, wide-eyed and with her mouth hanging open, as her five-year-old baby repeated to her a nine-year-old's demented and confused perspective of sex.

My mother was gasping for breath as she corrected the explanations. She felt five years old was a little too young to be discussing "the birds and the bees," but she couldn't let me grow up thinking sex was the collection of misinformation and science fiction I recounted to her. Looking back, I think this openness and knowledge about sex at a young age helped in my understanding of what happened to me later in life. I don't believe a child is ever too young to learn about human sexuality. Not every aspect, to be sure. But they need to know enough to protect themselves from sick individuals who will take advantage of a young person's willingness to trust adults. We will get more into that later.

Another value my mother consistently remarked on while raising all of us was the importance of telling the truth. Quite often, she would say, "You might get in trouble if you tell the truth, but not as much trouble as you will get in if you lie, and I will always catch you if you lie." She told us that our father knew everybody, and someone would see us if we did something wrong, and they would tell her, and that would be it. What "it" was, I still don't know because I was too scared to do anything wrong. I had been to the football games with my dad and honestly thought he knew everyone alive. By the time I was old enough to tell the difference, I was set in my ways. My mother also told us if we did something such as smoke, she would make us eat a whole pack of cigarettes. She also said if we smoked, we wouldn't be able to play sports, something she knew I loved. She threatened us with the fact that she would find out, and she would threaten us with things we cared about, such as sports. It was a good strategy to keep us straight, and I think it worked. Even when we would get in trouble, trouble was never as bad as it was supposed to be. She did a great job of raising four kids; I don't care what anybody thinks.

Finally, another effective strategy she used was to make us watch TV shows she felt would benefit us. She would then explain to us the morals and dilemmas faced by these characters on TV. I remember only the title of some of the movies, and I just remember the story of some. A lot of the time it was the after-school special such as *My Mom's Having a Baby*. That one was about—you guessed it—childbirth. Another was about two friends; one friend had Down Syndrome, and my mother explained Down Syndrome to us. Some were prime-time real-life stories such as *Something for Joey*, the story about John Cappelletti, the Heisman Trophy winner, and his brother who died of leukemia. She explained the whole situation to us because we were too young to understand then. Today, just thinking about John Cappelletti makes me realize what a wonderful thing he did by dedicating his Heisman Trophy to his dying brother, Joey. That's what life is all about: doing things to make other people happy. John Cappelletti is a hero, in my opinion.

Who knew that in 2004 I would stand on a stage at Penn State and accept an award for my accomplishments and resiliency? Ironically, Penn State would make worldwide headlines in 2011 with the Jerry Sandusky child sexual-abuse scandal. It was tough for me to watch that horrible situation unfold at a school that I love. Thankfully, the Paterno family released the *Clemente Report*, one of the most important documents regarding childhood sexual abuse I have ever read. It is unfortunate that so many people did not read it and still want to believe that Joe Paterno knew what Jerry Sandusky was doing. For me to believe that, I must believe my parents knew what Jeff Doucet was doing to me. I can promise you that my parents were much closer to me than the boys were to Joe Paterno. And I can promise you that my parents had no clue.

Because of the events that later occurred in my life, the movie that turned out to be the most important was *Fallen Angel*. It aired in 1981. I was eight or nine at the time. It was about child pornography. My mom sat me and Bubba down, and as the show progressed, she explained to us how people would use drugs or money or whatever to do "bad things" to children. If anyone ever did anything like that to us, we were to tell her, and she would stop that from happening. She said if that did happen, we were never to blame ourselves because grown-ups are stronger than children and should know better.

She also went on to explain child molesters—what they do and why. She explained that a boy in our neighborhood had been molested and killed, so we always had to let her know where we were. The one part my mother missed, and the one aspect she didn't realize at the time either, is that the sick monster, as she described, usually is not the dirty old man in the park molesting children, but it is a trusted friend of the family, someone in a position of trust, or even worse, a family member themselves.

I grew up afraid of three things: rats, snakes, and kidnappers. That's because my mother was also frightened of those three things. She instilled her fears in me. The funny thing is, the kidnapper I was afraid of was the kind that gets you in Kmart or the mall, not your karate teacher.

CHAPTER 5:

Karate

In the fall of 1982, the schools distributed flyers advertising karate classes that would take place after school. I thought nothing of it and threw the paper away. Mikey kept his and gave it to Mom. A friend of ours, Mark (we called him Markie) Boss, also gave the flyer to his mother. My mother and Mrs. Eileen (Markie's mother) were best friends and began to discuss the karate classes. They thought the classes might be something Mikey would be interested in, and it would help him with his coordination.

So Mom and Mrs. Eileen took the liberty of signing Mikey, Bubba, Markie, and me up for karate. The lessons were given at a local elementary school down the road from where we lived. After two or three sessions, the karate teacher never showed up again. We were told Rick (that was his name) took the money and split. We thought he was a big asshole, but he was a saint compared to the new guy . . .

A couple months after Rick split, we forgot all about karate. That is when we received a call from Jeff Doucet. He said the names of the students had been turned over to him by the organization who had arranged the makeup karate lessons, and he was going to finish up what we had paid for.

This was around November of 1982. In December, we had our first lessons under Jeff. We took a couple of classes, and Jeff told my mother and Mrs. Eileen that they had some fine kids with enormous potential. He told them he had a group of kids who fought in tournaments all over the South: Houston, Dallas, Florida, and a tournament in New Orleans that weekend. He said the "fighting team" always went to movies and maybe out for pizza. He asked my mother and Mrs. Eileen if we could go to the movies with them this weekend. My mother said she had to think about it.

My mother was not overprotective, but she was cautious. She called the Plauché Disaster Captain, Uncle Robert, and had him check Jeff's police record. The record, according to Uncle Robert, came back with nothing to cause concern. Only a few minor traffic tickets. So she felt it was safe and agreed to let us go.

We went to see the movie *They Call Me Bruce*. It was a karate movie that sort of poked fun at Bruce Lee. I thought it was stupid. After the movie, we went to Chuck E. Cheese's, where, oddly enough, my parents were attending a party for one of the younger children in the family. This was the beginning of Jeff gaining trust with my parents. They got to see the way he interacted with children. He appeared to be great with children—"just another child himself." What a "great" guy.

Jeff Doucet was born February 3, 1959. He was the son of Hayward and Elia Doucet. Jeff had three older brothers: Sam, Roland, and Mike. He had an older sister, Nelda, and a younger sister, Carline (later to be known as Terry). Jeff's father died when Jeff was a teenager.

Jeff's brother Sam was very hostile and enjoyed barrooms and fights. Sam spent a few years in Angola, the Louisiana State Penitentiary. Roland was the brother who, I feel, was closest to Jeff. He spent time in Vietnam and later got into the carpet business when he got back to the States. He seemed to be the most educated of all the Doucets. Mike, I don't know much about; I don't think Jeff was very close to him. All three brothers lived in Gonzales, Louisiana, when I knew Jeff.

Nelda, Elia, and Carline all lived in Port Arthur, Texas, at that time. I met them on a few occasions: once, when Sam and his wife were almost killed in a car wreck, and another, when we went to Port Arthur to visit.

Once, Carline told my mother that she was a lesbian because when she was younger, Elia used to whore her out to local degenerates. She got pregnant when she was thirteen and had a baby at fourteen.

Nelda told my mother that when Jeff was seventeen, he had been picked up for molesting a child. But it had been erased from his police record because Jeff's mother had a close relationship with someone in the department. There were other stories of Jeff potentially molesting other family members. This was all revealed to my mother *after* Jeff had taken me to California without her consent . . . I'm sure this really comforted her.

Jeff once told police officials that he had been sexually abused by three of his mother's boyfriends and said he "had great emotions and hatred for his mother because of it." When he was eight, living in Vinton, Louisiana, he had been sexually assaulted by his mother's boyfriend. Jeff said her boyfriend had been an alcoholic. Jeff claimed that for the year and a half this man and Jeff's mother had dated, this man had sexually abused him. About six months after the assaults started, Elia had walked in and witnessed the sexual abuse. Jeff said his mother had done nothing. She never even brought it up again.

Jeff said he and this boyfriend of his mother's had engaged in anal and oral sex for this eighteen-month period. This man had also had a friend named LT. Jeff said LT and his mother's boyfriend both spent time in Angola, the Louisiana State Penitentiary. LT also was alleged by Jeff to have molested him.

Jeff said he was ten years old when this first occurred, and he said that LT had also been dating Elia. This supposedly lasted a year.

Jeff then claimed that when he was fourteen, a guy named Tony had moved in with his mother. Jeff claimed that just like the previous two men, Tony had had a serious drinking problem. Tony had made sexual advances toward Jeff one day when his mother wasn't home. When Jeff had refused to consent to anal sex, he had been beaten. Tony had beaten him so badly that he hadn't been able to attend school for several days. He had then run away from home for a day.

When Jeff had returned, Tony had told Elia that the reason he had beaten Jeff was because Jeff had cursed him, so he'd had to "teach Jeff a lesson." Elia then sent Jeff away to Simi Valley, California, to live with his brother Roland. To me, this was unfair to Jeff, as this made him feel he was to blame, not Tony.

Jeff rarely talked about his mother to me. When he did, I could sense he didn't care for her. The police confession from March 16, 1984, substantiates my claim. It states that Jeff expressed an extreme hatred for his mother. He attributed his hatred to the fact that she, on more than one occasion, had walked in and observed him being sexually assaulted by three men she had dated, and she had done nothing to stop it; she had continued to date these men, allowing them to stay with her while they continued to sexually assault him. He stated that his mother never discussed it with him nor sought counseling for him. He also felt this was the reason he was attracted to children. This is bullshit.

This is a common misconception or myth about child sexual victimization. There are studies that have determined that 80–85 percent of incarcerated sex offenders claimed they had been molested as a child, but 50 percent of them failed the polygraph on that issue. Seems it was a convenient excuse.

Just recently, I was at a local Hooters, discussing this book with a friend. A waitress overheard our conversation and asked for more details. I told her I had been sexually abused for a year and then kidnapped. The young waitress then asked me, "Why didn't you tell? Are you attracted to males?"

My response was, "Absolutely not. I sucked a dick before, and I didn't like it."

By most people's account, Jeff Doucet was not a bad-looking man. He probably could have had any woman he wanted. Instead, he chose young boys around the age of ten or eleven. I happened to be one of what I assume was many.

Jeff was an excellent con man. He was as convincing as he was dishonest. If he had been honest and not attracted to kids, he could have been a very successful man. He was very smart. Regrettably, he used his brilliance to bring people down instead of up.

Jeff came up with some good business ideas but didn't execute them properly. He came up with the idea of an LSU bandana called a Tiger Rag. He sold the bandanas to Don Landers, the owner of a Baton Rouge convenient store called Cracker Barrel. Jeff had the rags made for one dollar, he sold them to Don Landers for two dollars, and Cracker Barrel sold them for three dollars. Free enterprise at work.

Eventually, Jeff was to deliver fifteen thousand bandanas to Don Landers. So Don gave Jeff fifteen thousand dollars up front and was to give him fifteen thousand more upon the delivery of the bandanas. Instead of buying the bandanas, Jeff bought a van with the first payment of the money. This left a supplier with fifteen thousand unwanted bandanas, and Don Landers was out fifteen thousand dollars. Landers pressed charges against Jeff and wanted his fifteen thousand dollars.

Jeff also came up with an idea to sell mugs with the final score of the LSU football games printed on them. A lot of people put in orders for the mugs, which called for the money up front. Jeff was unable to circumvent copyright laws and use LSU's mascot or name on the mugs. Some people canceled their checks, but Jeff continued to write his own. This left a trail of hot checks around Baton Rouge. A warrant was issued for his arrest on several charges. A lot of people wanted his ass.

In 1983, Jeff thought he had no option but to leave town to avoid prosecution. That is when he decided to go to California, and since I was his "favorite student," he decided I was going with him. Jeff probably would not have been caught if he hadn't taken me, but he did, and that was when the FBI got involved, because kidnapping is a much bigger crime than hot checks.

Most people think kidnapping is when a child is abducted—ironically, despite the name, it has little to do with taking a kid. It is only called kidnapping when a ransom is demanded. Otherwise it is called child abduction if a child is taken, or abduction or false imprisonment if an adult is taken. Since Jeff mentioned to my mother in a phone conversation while we were in California that "if you ever want to see Jody alive again, you will meet me in New York," his abduction turned into aggravated kidnapping, which he was charged with after his arrest.

Jeff was such a good con man . . . I feel this way because to me, that seemed to be all he knew. He had been raised with it and had seen it every day, and that is what he had learned. He didn't like to be alone; that is why he took me. His childhood had been taken away from him like so many others. He was sick. He had a mental disorder and paraphilia, and he never overcame his problem. I feel it was too late for him, and he never could have gotten over this sick pedophiliac attraction.

Sexologist John Money would have claimed Jeff had a "vandalized lovemap." A lovemap is a person's internal blueprint for their ideal erotic situations. A vandalized lovemap, according to Money, occurs when the lovemapping process becomes traumatized, as when a young child is either exposed to or forced to participate in such inappropriate behaviors as child sexual abuse, incest, or sexual sadomasochism. He states that such a lovemap is typically formed between the ages of five and eight. A vandalized lovemap may be paraphilic or hyposexual.

Jeff's eventual fate is nothing to celebrate or glorify. It was the final sad, regrettable event in a life filled with sad, regrettable events. I am going to try to give people an insight into how pedophiles think and act and what they are like. I do not hate Jeff for what he did; I have come to understand that he was sick and needed help. If blame is to be placed on anyone, it should be Elia. She failed Jeff. And in doing so, she helped make Jeff what he was. Jeff's life and death was the culmination of her failures. But I cannot cast judgment on Elia because I do not know her story. It might be just as complicated as Jeff's.

Sadly, there are many "Jeff Doucets" in this world today. The reason I am telling this story is for the benefit of others. Just like John Cappelletti, I want to give back. I don't want parents to experience the horrors my parents experienced, and I don't want children to have to go through the things I had to go through, because not every child will understand what is happening to them.

I was lucky; I understood, and I was able to handle it. Plus, I had an excellent support system. And trust me on this one—so did Daddy. Just go to YouTube and read the comments on the video of him—at the time of this writing, the video has over twenty million views. He still has staunch support.

I'm not saying that what I'm about to tell you doesn't affect me today, because it does. But I think it affects me in a positive way, not a negative one. I value companionship over sex. I value others and other's feelings over mine, and I have a general caring for the well-being of all of God's creations. So get ready. The story is about to begin.

CHAPTER 6:

The Fighting Team

Soon after karate classes resumed, Jeff moved the school to a building closer to my house. By being closer to the house, he got closer to the family. He would make the karate classes run longer and tell my mother he would bring us home. When he would bring us home, he would spend time talking to my parents . . . again, building their trust for him.

Also, when he would just bring us home, he would let each kid drive the 280ZX, a car he claimed as his, but really it belonged to some girl he claimed as his "girlfriend." It was a standard. Jeff would work the gas, clutch, and brake pedals, and we would steer. Every now and then Jeff would rest his hands in my lap, occasionally moving them. He would barely graze his hand over my private area. I thought, "It's no big deal. He just has to put his hands somewhere. It's not like he was playing with me or anything. It just makes me feel a little uncomfortable. Nothing to worry or really make a big deal about."

In March of '83, Jeff invited our team to go to Houston with him to watch a karate tournament. He said our fighting team would spend the weekend in Houston and go to AstroWorld before coming home. By this time, my parents trusted Jeff enough to let us go. They even talked with parents of other students about whether it was safe for us to go with Jeff, and those other parents even said he was "a great guy."

I didn't go to this first karate tournament that my brothers went to. I had an all-star basketball tournament in New Orleans that weekend. There was no way I was missing a basketball, baseball, or football game for no stupid karate. Those three sports were my first loves, and karate wasn't about to break up this romance.

Mikey and Bubba had a wonderful time on the trip to Houston. When they got back, I heard, "You should have been there" about one thousand times. They came back with great stories. There was a story about Monty, one of the kids on the fighting team, dipping Skoal snuff and getting sick to his stomach. There were stories of trashing hotels and pillow fights. And then the story of Mikey getting left at the gas station somewhere along Interstate 10 between Houston and Baton Rouge. Mikey got his first chance to ride in a police car when he was picked up, and surprisingly enough, he hasn't ridden in a police car since. (I would have never guessed that.) The trip sounded like so much fun that even my dad wanted to go on the next one.

Around this time, Jeff started spending more and more time with the family. He would come over on weekends and would usually end up spending the night. Every weekend back then, my aunts, uncles, and cousins would come over and talk and watch movies. The adults would play board games—usually Password. (Later it would become Trivial Pursuit.) Jeff would join in the games, play with the kids, and talk with my family. Jeff was becoming more like a part of the family. All of the family members were starting to trust Jeff.

In April 1983, our karate fighting team headed back to Houston along with my dad, Mikey, Bubba, and me. This time, however, I was ready to fight. We arrived Friday night and checked into the hotel, preparing for the tournament that was to take place Saturday.

I took second place in my division, which left me disappointed. I wanted to leave the tournament and go enjoy being on the town in Houston. Everybody else wanted to stay and watch the black belts fight, which was normal. They were the best. Not me; I wasn't that interested in karate. I wanted to see if the Astros were playing. So I told Jeff, "Let's go."

Boy, was that a mistake! He had been under the impression that I *loved* karate. I guess he got offended. Whatever it was, he sure started bitching at me. "If I would have known you'd rather do something else instead of karate, I would have left you at home." He went on and on, putting this guilt trip on me. "You are good. You're one of my best fighters. None of my students have ever gotten second place in their first tournament." I didn't know why he was so mad. I certainly didn't mean to make him that mad. I was beginning to feel guilty for ruining Jeff's trip.

That night we decided to go to the Galleria, an upscale mall in Houston, and go ice-skating. It was fun. Bubba would "check me against the boards" like the hockey players on ESPN. We would get going real fast (about three miles per hour) and slide on our stomachs across the ice. It was really good after the Zamboni machine had smoothed out the ice. We went home soaking wet but excited as hell.

When we slept on road trips, we all crammed into one or two rooms. About eight of us went on the trip, including my dad. Me, Bubba, another kid, and Jeff slept in one bed, and Mikey, my dad, and a couple of other kids slept either in the next bed or in an adjoining room. I had a tough time falling asleep that night because Jeff kept moving around and couldn't keep his hands to himself. He kept rubbing me, every now and then touching my private parts. I convinced myself, "He didn't mean anything by it; it was just an accident. I won't say nothing. I will just pretend to be sleeping and forget the whole thing ever happened. No reason to get my parents upset over a misunderstanding."

The next day, as promised, we went to AstroWorld. It was cold and dreary. We rode Thunder River and got soaked from the water. We froze our asses off all day long. Not to mention, all day long, I had white shorts on that you could see through, and a grown man, Jeff, was making comments about my frozen ass . . . "It was nothing; he's just kidding," I thought. "Forget it, and don't say anything. There is no need to get anyone alarmed. Plus, you know June will have a fit and blow everything out of proportion. He's cool."

We drove back to Baton Rouge and got in fairly late Sunday night. I went to school the next day, gloating that I had been to AstroWorld and my classmates had not. I told them how much fun I'd had and that they had missed it. I conveniently omitted that it had been cold, raining, and miserable, and I really hadn't had a good time. To them, it all sounded great.

The next weekend we were to have a crawfish boil out at Highland Road Community Park, which was about a mile away from the house. We would boil only the crawfish we were able to catch. That meant we needed to go catch some crawfish. Jeff knew of a great spot called Conway Bayou, under Airline Highway (US 61), near Sorrento. To a ten-year-old boy from Baton Rouge, setting crawfish traps on the bayou was almost as much fun as going to an LSU football game. The entire fighting team, all seven or eight of us, stayed in a hotel that Friday night.

That night, Jeff's rubbing was more aggressive. I stayed up all night, pretending to be asleep and hoping he would fall asleep, but he didn't. He rubbed my skin raw; it actually hurt, and that made me angry. The thought that kept going through my head over and over again was, "Why the hell won't he go to sleep? Now I know he wasn't accidentally doing it those other times. How can I get him to quit? This is driving me crazy. I have fun with him, but every time I lie down to go to sleep, here he comes, rubbing my dick. This has to stop!" I was only ten. I didn't know how to tell. I didn't want to distress the people I cared about.

Saturday we went to Sorrento, Louisiana, and caught a ton of crawfish. The thing I remember most about the trip is snakes, snakes, snakes. There were more snakes in that swamp than in *Raiders of the Lost Ark*. How we didn't get bitten by at least one of those snakes is beyond me. Looking back, we had no business being there with all those snakes. Hell, we should have just bought some crawfish; that would have been a lot quicker and a lot safer. I don't know if you have ever been in the swamps of Louisiana, but if you do go, then I advise you to take along some sort of protection or about fifty snakebite kits. But if you don't like snakes, just stay home. That was 1983, when alligators were a protected species. Now, I see alligator roadkill around that area where we went crawfishing. So there is no way I would go there again . . . never, unless I was with Troy Landry. #Chootem.

The crawfish boil went great. There were lots of people there. Sometime during the crawfish boil, Jeff volunteered to make a store run and asked if I could go with him. That was the only time he ever referred to me not telling my parents about what he did. I told him I had been asleep the night before and didn't know what he was talking about. That's what I tried to do—pretend nothing had happened. But he knew better.

He said, "You don't tell your parents what I do, do you?"

I said, "Do what?"

Jeff just left it at that, but he was about to become more daring with the things he did. I guess he knew right then he had me—that I hadn't told, and that I wouldn't tell if he made more advances toward me. And that is exactly what he did. He had tested my boundaries, and I guess I'd passed the test.

From time to time, Jeff would come over and visit. He would sneak to the back whenever I would take a bath. He wouldn't say much, but he would come into the bathroom, soap up his hand, and then masturbate me. Not all the way off. Just enough to physiologically arouse me. Jeff's sexual advances continued throughout the next year. I will discuss that in detail later. But for now, I am going to tell you a little more about the tactics he used to gain trust with the family. I'm not intending to drag this out, but it's important to illustrate the strategy that a pedophile will use to "groom" the parents of a child they want to or will sexually assault.

We had another tournament the next weekend. I would have won this one, but I kicked my opponent in the face (on accident) and was disqualified. I knocked him out. This trip was fun—much more so than the last trip. We went to AstroWorld again, and this time it wasn't cold and rainy. But the day I will never forget is Saturday, April 16, 1983. That was the first night Jeff performed oral sex on me.

During the ride back to the hotel from the tournament, Jeff whispered in my ear, "I'm gonna suck your dick tonight."

My first thought was, "Why would he want to do that? I pee out of that thing."

That night, after an old John Wayne movie went off the air and the other kids were asleep, Jeff ducked under the covers, like one of the snakes I am so afraid of, and began to perform oral sex on me.

It did not take me long to figure out why he wanted to do this; it felt wonderful. Now, don't confuse the physical pleasure with me enjoying the experience. My mind was thinking one thing while my body was reacting like a human body reacts. Never once in the year that Jeff was molesting me did I ever suggest he blow me because I was horny. This was just the next step in his progression. He would perform oral sex on me almost every day for the next month. That's when he said, "Now, I'm gonna fuck you." He said it as nonchalantly as if he were going to buy a newspaper or, more currently, check his Instagram.

Oh fuck, I thought. He was serious. I knew that he was going to fuck me, and thanks to a series of conversations with my mother about sexuality, I knew how he was going to fuck me. In short, I knew that was my ass . . . so to speak.

After that, he would perform oral sex on me every day, and after he was done with that, he would have sex with me anally. And this lasted from May 1983 throughout the kidnapping.

Many times, when a child is sexually abused, their bodies experience normal sexual pleasures, which leads to the child blaming himself or herself. But the body is going to do what the body does, so no victim of sexual abuse should feel guilty about that.

When school let out that summer, we began training for the pro-ams in July. This was the big national meet—the one we really wanted to win. It was to be held in Fort Worth, Texas, at the Tarrant County Convention Center.

We trained incredibly hard. Every day, we ran five miles, did five hundred sit-ups, did a thousand jumping jacks, stretched, and sparred. We were in the best physical condition of any ten- and eleven-year-olds in Baton Rouge. Jeff would also do stupid-ass things such as turning the heater on while we did our jumping jacks. It was ninety-eight degrees outside, and we had this pervert trying to kill us by turning on the heater. But, I repeat, we were in tremendous condition.

Finally, it was time to go kick some ass. We drove to Fort Worth with my family. My mother even made this trip because my uncle Jeff lived in Dallas, and my parents were going to stay with him and my aunt Carolyn.

We stayed at the Hilton right across from the Fort Worth Water Gardens. At this point in my life, it was the nicest hotel I had ever been in. Ray Charles was even staying there, and I was surprised at how short he was. It was a great thrill to see Ray Charles; he was the first famous person I ever got that close to. The day of the competition, I was dying to finally use the skills I had developed. All the hard work, the sweat, the tears, and all the other bullshit in my life would soon disappear for at least a little while. In retrospect, it's ironic that out on that mat, facing a highly trained martial artist bent on destroying me, was where I felt safe. No one could touch me. No one could have beaten me this day . . . and no one did.

I took out a great deal of pent-up frustration that day. No one in that arena had any idea what drove me to fight like I did. The first match set the tone. It let all the other fighters know that on that day, anybody wanting to be the national champion in this age group, in this division, was going to have to beat Jody Plauché to do it. I hit my opponent with the first punch, a ridge hand (my favorite and probably most powerful punch), and he fell to the floor, crying. I got a warning from the referee. "Don't throw your ridge hand that hard again, or you are disqualified," he said.

I thought to myself, "Who are you to tell me how to fight? I might be young, but I'll kick your ass too."

Now I couldn't use my favorite punch because I could not throw it lightly. So I reversed my stance and threw a crushing back fist to the same spot on the back of his head. Again, he fell, crying and holding his head. And again, I got warned for hitting too hard.

"I told you not to hit that hard," said the referee.

I immediately responded, "You said don't hit him with a ridge hand that hard; that wasn't a ridge hand."

The battered kid finally staggered back to his feet. By now, he was very unsteady and moving really slowly. He was worn out. That was when I knew I could use my favorite move, the sliding sidekick. Executed correctly, it has tremendous force and power. I never had the misfortune of being on the receiving end of a sliding sidekick, but I bet it hurts. It sure seemed to hurt this poor guy. Because for the third time in about forty-five seconds, he was on the floor. He didn't have enough hands to hold all the aching parts of his body.

The score was four to nothing. Two points for kicks, and one point for hand strikes. All I needed was one more point. Just to make the ref happy and give the kid a break (also to humiliate him in front of everybody else . . . on that day, I admit, I was not the nicest person), I threw the softest back fist that barely landed, giving me a point and the win.

This pissed him off. Now he wanted to kick my ass for humiliating him. He figured that fighting with the score and refs and those kinds of things may not work, and he may have just lost, but to redeem himself in front of his peers, he was going to kick my ass. As I started to walk off the mat, I could see him looking at me. He was huffing and puffing, with tears welling up in his eyes. I could tell he hadn't quite had his fill. When I turned my back, I heard him charge at me. I was ready for him. I pivoted quickly and threw a sidekick that lifted him off the ground.

He let out this horrible-sounding noise, one I had never heard before. His teammates and coaches came running on the floor and carried him off, setting him on the ground to the side of the ring. I went and sat by my cousin Brad, who had watched the whole thing. With this worried sound in his voice, Brad said, "You better go check on that guy."

I simply said, "Fuck him. He'll be okay."

I went on to pretty much massacre everybody else except my last opponent in the championship match. I knew I could annihilate him, but he never gave me the opportunity. He ran the whole time. Neither one of us could score a point. Finally, after he stepped out of the ring for about the tenth time, I was awarded a point. I chased him around for a few more seconds, and then the timekeeper yelled, "Time!"

Nobody heard her, and we continued to fight. About ten seconds later, in my mounting frustration, I stepped into him, and he threw a front kick that actually landed. He was initially awarded two points for a good kick. I got upset because I thought I'd lost.

The timekeeper then informed the refs that the match had in fact been over before the kick had landed.

When I was told I won, I was confused and so was the guy I was fighting. Then they explained it. I wanted to redo the whole match. Instead, they just gave me the first-place plate, which was to go on the first-place trophy that I had to go pick up.

I walked over to the trophy area to pick up my trophy. Lo and behold, my opponent in the championship match was picking up his trophy at the same time. He kept staring at me. I was initially content to ignore him. But finally, I had enough. I glared back at him.

He eventually worked up the nerve to say, "You know I beat you, don't you?"

This chapped my ass. I thought to myself, "I would have kicked your little skinny ass if you wouldn't have run!" But instead, I told him, "Okay, you got the second-place plate, and I got the first-place plate. Nobody is here. No time limit, no points. If you want to prove to me you deserve the first-place trophy, go ahead."

He accepted his second-place trophy with grace and didn't say another word after that.

After the tournament, we all went back to the hotel. My cousin Brad came back to the hotel with us. My parents went back to Dallas, leaving

Brad to spend the night with his cousins he rarely got to see.

That night, Jeff popped Brad on the back of the head just like he used to do to us. But Brad didn't know Jeff. Brad wasn't "one of us," so Brad called my uncle Jeff. This report really pissed my uncle off. He said he didn't care what kind of karate Jeff knew; he was going to kick his ass.

Nothing ever happened between the two Jeffs. But the next day, Jeff Doucet was supposed to drop us off with my parents. In keeping with our history, he laid another a guilt trip on me (as if I could tell my parents, "I'm going with Jeff, not you"). When Jeff told me bye, he kissed me on the mouth. This was something he always did.

Uncle Jeff saw this and became alarmed. He told my parents, "That's not right. A grown man shouldn't be kissing a little boy on the mouth like that."

My parents said, "Oh, Jeff, you just have to *get to know him*. He's really a great guy. You're just still mad over what happened last night. He didn't mean to hurt Brad; he always does that."

I guess sometimes it takes an outsider looking in to see what's really going on. For example, you could work on a crossword puzzle all day, get a mental block, and never come up with a four-letter word starting with *D* that stands for a bird that swims in water and also sounds like a slang term for sex. Unless someone new comes along and says, "Duck," you could sit there all day and never figure it out. You then look back on the situation and say, "I should have known that. It was so obvious." But chances are, you could then go on and finish the crossword puzzle. But within the crossword-puzzle scenario, you don't have a guy who has spent weeks, months, or years convincing you he's the best guy on earth and diverting your attention elsewhere.

In life, just as you would with the crossword puzzle, you need to move ahead and not dwell on the fact that you couldn't figure that out. Too many people, in my opinion, spend the rest of their lives disappointed because they "couldn't figure out the word *duck*." They dwell on past mistakes instead of learning from them and moving on.

So, in life, if you screw up and fail to recognize right word, "duck it," and move on with your life. It's just another piece of the puzzle that will contribute to your life story.

Uncle Jeff was right. Something was terribly wrong. But because my parents "knew" and trusted Jeff Doucet, they couldn't see it. They had been well manipulated and deceived by him. Uncle Jeff had not. Because of that, he was not trusting and misled by his front. But no one would listen to him; they had to learn for themselves.

We spent the rest of that week in Dallas, swimming, riding bikes, fishing, and playing in the woods. Mom would have killed us if she'd found out we were playing in the woods. Eventually she did find out because when we got back to Baton Rouge, Bubba and I came down with the worst case of poison ivy. It was so bad we had to go see *Dr. Miller*. We hated going to see Dr. Miller because we knew we were getting a shot. We did go, but to this day, I haven't contracted poison ivy again.

About a month later, we had a local tournament to fight in. The night before, we went to another karate school and sparred with other kids we didn't know. It was kind of unfair because it was two on one. One of their guys versus one of Jeff's students who was accompanied by another student from the other gym.

When my turn came up, I felt sorry for the one guy fighting alone. I decided I would take it easy and not hit this guy. That was, until he decided to hit me. After that I teed off on him.

In tournaments, you were not allowed to hit in the face, but this day we were. I hit this kid square in the face. And to my surprise, he hit me back, right in my face. Now I was mad. I hit him about ten more times in the face until they made us stop.

The next day at the tournament, the guy's karate teacher brought him up to Jeff and showed him the inside of his mouth. It was all blue and cut up. I knew that guy didn't want any more of me.

When competition rolled around, I knew I would win. Hell, I was national champ. These local guys didn't stand a chance. The first round I was sitting there, watching this one guy fight. He was kind of chubby, but he hit like a mule. He demolished his opponent. I couldn't wait to fight him. The second round, he fought this skinny black kid nicknamed "Super Foot." That was what his cheering section called him. He hit Super Foot and knocked him down twice. The score was two to zero. In this tournament, the winner was the first fighter to three points, and a kick or a punch counted as one point.

Down by two points, Super Foot was pissed. He huffed, puffed, and growled; then he executed a flying sidekick and kicked Ol' Chubby right in his gut. The kick left Chubby unable to breathe. This allowed Super Foot to kick him two more times to come back and win. The funny thing was that Super Foot did that in his first fight and then in his next two as well. It was one of the funniest things I'd ever seen.

I wanted to fight Super Foot so bad, just so I could kick his super-footed ass. Luckily for me, I got the chance in the final match. The first point, I clobbered Super Foot with a ridge hand, knocking him down. The second point, I hit him with another ridge hand, making him cry.

The fans were cheering, "Go Super Foot! Go Super Foot!" Little did they know, it was about to be Super Foot's ass. As expected, Super Foot huffed, puffed, and growled. He took off charging at me, leaped into the air, and met Mr. Sidekick. Super Foot looked more like Superman flying across the ring, hitting his head on the floor. Super Foot had to be carried from the ring. As for his fans, they didn't like me very much. I had exposed their Super Foot for the mere mortal that he was.

Besides fighting and training, Jeff would take us to the movies. We would walk around the mall, cut up, start trouble, and basically act like kids. We would go to the skating rink and act like heathens, looking for a fight. We never started them; we just looked for them. We never got in a fight with anybody on the street. We came close once. We were at the skating rink, and this guy was messing with these two girls. Being the "heroes" that we were, we went to help the girls. We tried to run him off. But the guy kept smarting off to us. He was really being a dick. But then he quit when he realized about seven karate guys were about to change his outlook on life and how to treat women. We calmly started to take off our skates—that way we could kick. Then he started apologizing. First to the girls, and then to us . . . for the inconvenience.

There was this one time we were riding around in Baton Rouge in the Old Goodwood subdivision, near Independence Park and the main library. We saw this kid playing football by himself in his front yard. Jeff turned the car around, and we jumped out. All seven of us ran up to him, hollering and screaming. We shook him and knocked the football out of his hands and ran around him in a circle twice. Then, as suddenly as it had started, we just stopped. We all calmly walked back to the car, and Jeff drove off as if nothing had happened. The poor kid was scared as shit. He didn't know what to do. He just stood there, completely stunned by what had just happened. And probably scared for his life. My cousin Aaron later went to high school with this guy. I got to meet him once, and we just laughed at the whole thing.

That whole summer, the fighting team stuck together, traveled together, and spent most of our time together. We went on TV, talking about the LSU mugs we were trying to sell. It was funny because we went on a local television talk show at eight o'clock in the morning called *Morning in Louisiana*, after which a children's show called *The Buckskin Bill Show* aired.

The Buckskin Bill Show aired for decades in Baton Rouge. Buckskin Bill was basically Baton Rouge's version of Mr. Rogers. Kids in town would mail in their birth dates, and Buckskin Bill would read them over the air. Every Monday, he would do the "Monday Morning March." He would announce that it was time for the Monday Morning March, and every child watching in Baton Rouge knew what that meant. As the Sousa-style march music played, he would march around the set, holding a baton, while the kids at home did the same.

Mom can't recall the number of times she and Bubba "Monday Morning Marched" around the den with a baton. Well, this was every kid from Baton Rouge's dream. After we did the talk show at eight o'clock in the morning, we watched Buckskin Bill do the march, and he invited us to join in. Our parents, sitting at home and talking about the show we had just been on, were shocked to see their precious babies marching around like fools with Buckskin Bill. But my mother was a little disappointed because Bubba was not there to do the Monday Morning March with us. Thank you sincerely, Buckskin Bill, for making that day special for me.

Also, we got to meet the lieutenant governor at the time, Bobby Freeman. Jeff conned him into endorsing his products (Tiger Rag and the LSU mugs). Lieutenant Governor Freeman was probably humiliated later for having been in a business deal with a con man like Jeff. I feel for Bobby; he was only trying to do the right thing and help out some local kids. But Jeff was an asshole and didn't care whom he hurt or humiliated. He would lie to and try to con the Dalai Lama, the Pope, and Oprah Winfrey if he could. I think that's why I care so much for other people. I know that's why I hate lying so much.

To most people, Jeff was this remarkable guy. He taught kids discipline and hung out with them. He took them to do fun activities. He just seemed to be a trustworthy guy. My parents and everybody who ever came across Jeff Doucet, including the lieutenant governor, thought that he was great for kids. The *Morning Advocate* and the *State Times* even published articles describing Jeff's virtues as a karate instructor and explaining how he was providing local children the opportunity to run a business. The local news on WBRZ, Channel 2, even did a story on us. To everybody on the outside, it all just *seemed* so perfect . . .

CHAPTER 7:

Off to Disneyland

As the new year, 1984, approached, Jeff began talking about leaving Baton Rouge. He would tell me he was sick of the town and would like to get away. He talked fondly about the time he had once briefly lived with his brother in California as a teen. He really enjoyed talking about going to California.

My mother would tell me about people calling and looking for Jeff because he had written another hot check. I almost got in trouble one time for forging my mother's name on the back of some checks and cashing them at the grocery store down the street.

Jeff would make me forge my mother's name on a check, tell me it wasn't good enough, and have me sign another and go cash it. What he would later do without my knowledge was also cash the one that I had supposedly forged unsatisfactorily. Though I only cashed two checks myself, I probably signed ten. This was one of the reasons there was a warrant issued for his arrest. I knew there was more incentive behind Jeff wanting to leave Baton Rouge other than his excuse that he just "wanted to get away."

As I mentioned earlier about the bandanas and the mugs, Jeff was supposed to appear in court because Don Landers was suing him for the money he had advanced Jeff. The court date was scheduled for March 14, 1984. (Don't ask me why I remember.) To avoid prosecution, Jeff would have to be prepared to repay ten thousand dollars. Ten thousand dollars Jeff did not have.

As February neared, Jeff spoke of going to California more and more frequently. He eventually confided in me concerning the real reason he needed to leave Baton Rouge.

"There's no way I can get the money," he admitted. "But when I leave, I'm taking you with me."

I did not object. Frankly, it wasn't because I was afraid. I felt I had no real choice to refuse. I knew the man was sick, and I knew that if I said no, he would freak out. I wouldn't even allow myself to speculate about what he might have done. I just knew I was not going to take that chance of finding out.

A couple weeks later, Jeff made his decision to leave. I knew about it because Jeff had been telling me it was a possibility. I knew I was going with him, and I knew it was soon; I just didn't know exactly when.

Then, on February 19, 1984, at nine o'clock in the morning, Jeff arrived at our house. He knocked on the door and, as usual, was invited in. He told my mother that his brother had dropped him off and was going to a friend's house to lay some carpet. Jeff asked my mother if he could borrow her car so he could drive up there to check on his brother and make sure everything went smoothly. These days, he could have just taken an Uber or Lyft to go check on the carpet.

The truth is, his brother never dropped him off. Also, there was no carpet-install job to check on. In fact, I don't think Jeff had talked to his brother in a couple of weeks at this point. The brothers had argued, and Jeff had been tossed out of his brother's apartment. Jeff had since been sleeping in the storeroom outside of our house at night.

Mom had no idea any of this was going on. He slept in the storeroom for two weeks before he took me to California. A couple of days before he took me, my mother asked me if I knew where Jeff was staying. I lied. I told her I had no idea and asked why she was questioning me on this. She said, "Never mind; it's nothing."

Mom did suspect that he might have slept there at least one night because he left the blankets I had given him on the floor of the storeroom. She would have killed me if she had known. She was separated and planning on getting a divorce. Consequently, she was concerned about how it would appear to the court that a man had been sleeping there. Understandably, she was worried that someone would think she and Jeff had a romantic relationship. As we know, there was nothing romantic about their relationship. Still, she was afraid she could lose custody of her children. After her initial investigation, she didn't bring it up again.

He took the car keys from my mother. He thanked her, as a polite person would. Just before Jeff left the house, he called out to me, as he had a hundred times before, "Jody, come ride with me."

I had an idea this might be it. But I couldn't be sure. We got in the car. He turned the ignition. And above the sound of the motor and chattering radio, Jeff removed any doubt that remained.

"We are going to California."

I was numb. I'd always had hope he would never leave, but now the reality had set in—we were on our way.

The first leg of his trip was to his brother Mike's house to pick up a few of his things. Then onto Interstate 10, heading west for Port Arthur, Texas. On the drive, across the Atchafalaya Basin Bridge, I looked over and saw a friend and a classmate, Kristie Schexnayder. She unknowingly became an eyewitness to my abduction turned kidnapping. Just like that, in broad daylight, in my mother's own car, Jeff had taken me.

We reached Port Arthur on Sunday and stayed until Tuesday morning. Meanwhile, my mother was completely distraught. Panic stricken, she called Jeff's mother and asked if we were there. Elia told her we were. My mother then told Elia that Jeff had kidnapped me. She told Elia that she was going to call the police if I wasn't returned immediately.

Jeff lied to Elia, saying he was planning to return me to Baton Rouge and head to New York, and he needed money to do so. He then drove us to Vinton, Louisiana. There, we visited an uncle of Jeff's so he could ask for a loan to get to New York. I think the uncle gave him some money, but I'm not sure.

Somehow, Jeff collected enough money for two bus tickets to Los Angeles, California. We went to the bus station in Orange, Texas. Jeff was anxious to leave. Elia was still under the impression that Jeff was going to New York and was dropping me off in Baton Rouge on the way.

Elia did have knowledge that Jeff had me against my mother's will. As far as I can tell, Elia in no way helped Jeff take me to California. First, she didn't want her son charged with kidnapping, and secondly, she really was looking after my well-being. I feel in no way, shape, or form that Elia did aid and abet in the kidnapping. Jeff lied to her—she didn't have a clue.

The bus trip to Los Angeles was long. We stopped off in several places to drop off and pick up passengers. One place that stood out to me was El Paso, Texas. I remember seeing lights and lights and lights. It was incredible.

Jeff was making friends with the old ladies on the bus. He was himself. He was funny, telling jokes and stories. He charmed them, like always. He deceived them, like always. And they loved him . . . like always. He told them I was his son and that we were moving to California so he could find work.

Also, in El Paso, the police escorted an escaped mental patient off the bus. She still had her hospital armband on. Being a mental patient wasn't what got her kicked off the bus, though. That had more to do with the fact that she apparently had been giving blow jobs all night long. I was asleep, so I didn't get mine, but I heard the stories the next morning.

Then came a stop in Tucson, Arizona. We had lunch, and Jeff shaved his beard. He was afraid of the border patrol. He was convinced that once we passed them, we would be just fine.

His old lady friends were curious as to why he shaved his beard because he "looked so handsome with it." He told them (this is a smooth one) that the job he was getting probably wouldn't allow facial hair. To be proactive and not make it necessary for his employer to ask him to shave it, he decided he would save them the trouble and do it now.

They thought that was a brilliant idea.

Then came Phoenix. I remember Phoenix because it was so beautiful, so clean, and was surrounded by mountains. If you've ever been to Phoenix, you know how beautiful it is.

After we left Phoenix, Jeff met this girl, Leah. I had fallen asleep, but when I woke up, they were making out. He was going at it. My first reaction was complete shock, and then (I'm really ashamed to admit this) I got jealous. I got pissed. Real pissed. Almost to the point where I can't explain it. I curled up on the seat and tried to go back to sleep, but I couldn't. I just couldn't.

Looking back, I'm willing to bet that as he had her attention focused on the lip-lock he had her in, his free hand was digging through her purse. She was pretty. But she was being played for a fool.

Jeff made two comments about her to me.

First, "She has a disease." (Don't ask me why he would say that; I still don't know.)

Then he said, "Do you want to fuck her?"

Common sense should have told him if she had a disease I didn't want to fuck her. I knew she didn't have a disease, and I did want to fuck her, but I had to tell him no. That way he wouldn't get mad, and I wouldn't have to hear his bullshit about not loving him.

Actually, the thought of being with a girl was appealing. I didn't know how long I was stuck being his plaything, and I figured I might as well get it when I could.

The next thing I remember was waking up in Los Angeles, looking at skid row. I had never seen that many people in my life, let alone people sleeping on the streets. I may have been young, but my heart went out to those people. My situation seemed like nothing next to theirs: homeless, hungry, and sleeping on the streets.

At least I had food, a place to stay, and parents who loved me. These people had nothing. Whenever I think that everything is going bad for me and nothing is going right, I always think of the ones less fortunate than me. They are usually the inspiration behind the things I do.

That Thursday we arrived in Los Angeles around two o'clock in the morning. We stayed in the bus station until about seven, then went to get a bite to eat. We walked around downtown LA most of the day.

At one point, we saw a bunch of cops blocking off the street. Jeff got nervous, but I knew something he didn't. They were filming a movie.

This was LA; this was where they filmed movies, and I wanted to go check it out. I had seen part of the filming for *The Toy*, a movie starring Richard Pryor and Jackie Gleason, which had been filmed in Baton Rouge about a year before, so I knew what the situation looked like.

Well, they weren't filming a movie—they were filming a segment of *Hill Street Blues*. Which, at the time, was Jeff's favorite TV show. We stayed there for a couple of hours, watching them do the same scene over and over. We got some autographs and found out it would be airing March 15. (In 1992, I saw that show and the scene; I had chills going all the way up my body. It was so weird seeing it again after all those years. I was mad I didn't get it on tape. Then about six months later, I was at a friend's house, and it came on again. This time I got it on tape. It was still real weird seeing it again.)

Now Jeff began to worry. We were in Los Angeles, California, we didn't know anybody, and we were out of money. Who could he con now? I was even starting to worry. But with only a few cons left in him, he came up with probably the biggest and best one of them all.

He used the last few dollars we had to buy a karate magazine. He looked in the back for a name he recognized. Sure enough, he found one. Al Garza out of Houston would be his next victim. Jeff knew Al from karate tournaments. They weren't good friends, but they were acquaintances. As I stated earlier, when I had been disqualified, it had been at one of Al's tournaments because I had accidentally kicked one of his students in the eye, knocking him out.

Jeff called Al and told him that he and a few of his best fighters had taken a karate trip to Los Angeles and that the van we had used had been stolen. He told Al that if he could wire us six hundred dollars, we could get home, and he would pay him back. Al did not hesitate to send the money. We picked it up—$550—that evening at Western Union, "the fastest way to send money." (At least in 1984, it was.)

I would now like to apologize to Al for what happened. I would also like to thank him for what he did. If it hadn't been for Al's generosity, there is no telling what would have happened to me. Remember, Jeff knew how to raise money because he had seen how his mother did it when he was younger. We were in California, and I'm sure he could have found someone who would have paid money to sleep with a young boy. Jeff hadn't mentioned this so far, but it would only be a matter of one week before he asked me what I thought about the idea. When he did, I told him I wanted no part of it, not even for him. He didn't cause much of a commotion then because I had set the limit. There was no way—not me. Yeah, right. Jeff would have done it, and there would have been nothing I could have done about it. To think it only would have been for a couple of bucks.

We stayed at the Hilton in downtown Los Angeles that night for I think eighty dollars. Not the smartest way to spend limited funds, but they don't teach money management in sixth grade (both of our education levels). I still knew that was stupid.

The next day we took a bus to Canoga Park. Jeff looked around for a cheap apartment and a job. Nada. Nothing. Nobody was hiring a fugitive child molester on the run with a sixth grade education. So we went back to LA and took a bus to Anaheim, California.

We arrived that night, grabbed something to eat, and settled into what wasn't a "good night's sleep." I guess with money in his pocket, and feeling somewhat safe, Jeff was in the mood. He hadn't been in the mood most of the "trip," but that night he was. I think deep down in his sick mind, he thought he was running in a marathon because it seemed to last all night. It was really pissing me off because I was tired, and I wanted to be rested up because we were going to Disneyland the next day.

Jeff wanted to do some freaky shit that night. He wanted me to do him up the ass. This wasn't happening, thank God, for some reason, and I don't know why, but I just wasn't turned on looking at his hairy ass. I couldn't even think of anyone else. (Note: I wrote this last sentence in 1993—had I written it today, I would have included a "winky face" to highlight the sarcasm.)

Finally, the next morning we went to Disneyland, "The Happiest Place on Earth." To me, it was. I knew I was safe. We rode Space Mountain, Pirates of the Caribbean, and It's a Small World. We ate chocolate-covered frozen bananas and at a Cajun restaurant for a down-South, home-cooked meal. It wasn't. It was the worst bowl of gumbo I had ever eaten. Years later, on Facebook, I would see a video on "How to make Disney gumbo." That explained a lot.

Now that the dream was over, we checked into the Samoa Motel, room 38. Thirty-eight was Jeff's unluckiest number by far. Jeff was superstitious and was afraid of the number thirteen; he should have avoided thirty-eight. Daddy was thirty-eight when he shot Jeff with a .38-caliber revolver.

While staying at the Samoa, a lot of interesting things happened. Jeff dyed my blond hair black, shaved his mustache, and pretty much let me come and go as I pleased. I did a lot of swimming and sitting in the hot tub.

While I would be swimming, Jeff would be inside. I'm not sure what he was doing. Watching TV or talking on the phone with my mother. After we had been gone a week, Jeff finally told me to call home. It was Sunday night when I called. I said, "Hey," and I heard Mom say, "Hey, baby," still groggy from the little sleep she had finally gotten.

That Tuesday when Jeff and I had left the bus station in Orange, Texas, my mother and Uncle Robert arrived in Port Arthur, looking for me. They were a little too late. That was when my mother found out—from Nelda, Jeff's sister—all the horror stories about Jeff molesting children.

Uncle Robert already had come to that conclusion and was prepared to kill Jeff on sight.

They contacted Mike Barnett, a major with the Baton Rouge Police Department, a friend of the family, and a guy my mother had dated after high school. He contacted the FBI, and they put a wire on our phone lines back home. Mike was my mother's coach through each of the phone conversations. He listened in on another line and would write things down for my mother to ask. He did an outstanding job keeping my mother cool. Jeff had no clue they were listening in.

Jeff kept insisting we were in New York. He kept telling my mother to meet him there with the other three kids. Once, they asked Jeff the time, and he replied that it was five o'clock, which was the time in LA. That translated to seven o'clock in Baton Rouge and eight o'clock in New York. Jeff, being the uneducated piece of shit (sorry, I had to get it out) that he was, said it was five o'clock. I told him to say the clock was broken, and that it was eight o'clock, since we were supposedly in New York. He did, but it was too late.

Another dumb thing he did was let me tell them we saw the filming of *Hill Street Blues*. Peggy Graham, a good friend, got on the phone, called Hollywood, and asked where they filmed *Hill Street Blues*. They told her mostly in Los Angeles and sometimes in Chicago. But most recently in LA.

The scent was getting strong, and Jeff's days were numbered.

One day while we were in Anaheim, Jeff took me to the mall. Another day he left me there all day. From about eight in the morning until about eight that night. He went to Fullerton to look for a job and to get a driver's license. Elia had given Jeff a copy of his brother Mike's birth certificate, and he was going to use that as his identification. By doing this when he was on the run with me, she aided and abetted in my abduction. In 1984, Jeff was an innovator of identity theft.

The next few days, Jeff talked to my mother more and more. Finally, we were running out of money. Jeff had paid for our hotel room for one week, and time was running out. We had a few more days left to stay, but the pocket money was low.

Jeff then made his fatal mistake. I'm not sure whether he did it out of ignorance or out of necessity, but he had me call home collect. When I did, my mother asked the operator for "time and charges." As soon as the phone call was over, the operator came back on the line, told her how much the call cost, how long it was, where it came from, the address, and the room number. They had him.

Mike Barnett called the Anaheim police, and they headed for the Samoa Motel (now known as Americas Best Value Inn and Suites) at 425 West Katella Avenue, Anaheim, California, room 38. The funny story we found out later was that the first time the police busted into a hotel room looking for us, they were at the wrong room.

Jeff had called my mother back and was talking to her when we heard a knock on the door. Then we heard a key turning, and what seemed like fifty police officers came busting into the room. They pointed loaded guns at me, at him, and at anything that looked like it was moving. Jeff immediately put the phone down and got into the frisk position on the wall.

An officer walked across the room and told Jeff, "I ought to punch you right in the fucking mouth." This was the last time I ever saw Jeff. The other officers then took me out of the room as they read Jeff his rights. When they got me outside, they began asking me questions. And the questioning would last most of the night.

First, they asked my name, then Jeff's. They asked if blond was the color of my hair and why Jeff dyed it black. I played dumb and said, "I don't know." I really wanted to say, "Why do you think, dumb ass?"

They were nice to me, but I was still mad at them. They had arrested my friend and taken me away from him. I knew I would be questioned all night long. "Did Jeff ever touch you? Did Jeff ever make you touch him?" I wasn't in the mood to sit there all night and lie. Which was exactly what I was going to do.

When we got to the police station, I was proved right. They interrogated me for two hours. I stood by my story. I told the truth except for the one lie. They were getting mad because they couldn't get to me. I wouldn't crack. I couldn't crack. I knew the next stop would be the hospital to get me checked out. I was right again.

Two officers escorted me to the hospital, where a complete physical examination was performed. They took my blood and asked me questions about every scar I had. The funny thing was I had to use the bathroom bad (to pee). When the doctor told me to pull down my pants, I was about to explode. Then the doctor started pushing on my bladder, causing a few drops to come out.

She asked me, "Does fluid usually leak out of your penis like this?"

I told her, "When I have to pee this bad and somebody pushes on my stomach, it does."

She left the room, and I left a large urine sample for them to analyze later. I filled up the whole thing and had to get another bottle to pee in. It felt so good to relieve that pressure. You know I had to pee bad if I remember it this many years later.

After I finished, the doctor came back. She had a long plastic glove with Vaseline caked on. The glove went all the way up her arm, and this scared me. Jeff was big but was no comparison to somebody's arm.

She then told me to bend over. I knew the position well, but you never get used to it, and you definitely never enjoy it. She then stuck her finger or arm (I couldn't tell; I don't have eyes in the back of my head) up my ass. Then she reamed me with two foot-long cotton swabs.

Finally, it was over. I knew once the specimens came back positive, I could quit lying. But until then, the story was that Jeff never touched me. I also was happy to know that this was going to be the last time anybody ever stuck anything up my ass. Boy, what a relief!

Next on the police agenda was the Albert Sitton Home (which closed in 1985, and they opened a new building across the street called the Orangewood Children's Home, now called the Orangewood Children and Family Center) for protective custody. I got there close to three or four in the morning. They took my clothes, made me shower, and put me in some of their rags. They escorted me to a room with about forty beds, most of which were full of children just like myself, and gave me a bed. Finally, some sleep.

At eight o'clock the next morning, the counselors were waking everybody up, including me. I wasn't going for that one bit. I told them, "Leave me alone. I just got here, and I'm not staying."

One counselor had been informed about me and said, "That's right; he got here around four o'clock this morning. Let him sleep."

Then, while the other kids ate breakfast, they sat around talking about Michael Jackson winning all kinds of Grammy Awards the night before, and they talked about him taking off his glasses for the girls in the balcony. Usually I would be glad to join in on a conversation about my favorite singer and performer, but not when it was keeping me awake. Finally, I got pissed off and joined the other kids for breakfast because either way, I couldn't sleep with them talking.

While everyone was at the school that was provided, I sat around watching *Rocky III*. That's when someone told me I needed to go talk to a social worker. I walked to the main building and sat in the waiting room, where *Superman* was showing. I dozed off right before they told me I had to go get a physical. I seriously objected. I told them I'd just had a physical a few hours ago, and there was no need for another one.

All they did was take my blood pressure and check out my mouth to see if I had a sore throat. No gloves, no wonder jelly (which isn't so wonderful), and no foot-long cotton swabs. So that physical wasn't so bad. I had heard about the physicals where the doctors told you to cough, and since my nurse was an attractive blonde, I was kind of hoping she would do it. But to my disappointment, it wasn't that kind of physical.

After that I got to meet with my social worker. At the time I thought he was the biggest dick-face alive. He seemed to be blaming me for leaving with Jeff. I couldn't tell him I had no choice, so he kept blaming me. He really pissed me off. I wanted to karate chop his ass. Maybe then he would know not to blame me.

I left there, and it was playtime. All the kids were out on the playground. I went and sat off by myself, looking all sad and pitiful. I just wanted to get back home so this could all be over. This lady came up to me and said, "What's the matter? You look like you just lost your best friend. Do you want to talk about it?"

I told her no. She had made a good guess. I felt as though I *had* lost my best friend—Jeff.

When I picked my head up, I saw some guys playing basketball, my favorite sport. So I casually walked over and began to watch. This one guy thought he was good, and nobody wanted to play him one on one. I did. I could play basketball, and I knew I could whup his ass.

Sure enough, I dusted him. I felt as though I looked like Michael Jordan playing those little kids in the Gatorade commercials. Everyone thought I was Dr. J. They came over and watched me humiliate this guy. He was "the man" when it came to basketball, and this new guy was schooling him. After that, I felt better and began socializing with everyone else. They loved me.

The two guys I remember most were these two black kids who went by MJ and TC. TC was close to my age, and MJ was probably the oldest kid there. MJ impressed me because he was so nice. All the little kids would go to MJ like he was their big brother. He accepted the role and was one of the nicest guys I had ever met. The way he treated them earned my respect. I don't know what happened to them or why they were in there, but whatever happened, I'm willing to bet that MJ is a good father to someone out there.

When nine o'clock rolled around, I was exhausted. I was about to go to bed when someone told me I would be leaving at 1:10 a.m. out of LAX (Los Angeles International). I lay down only to be awoken by some people saying, "Come on; let's go get your stuff so you can go home."

This man drove me to the airport. We got along great. He told me the news media had gotten wind of the story and wanted to film me leaving for home at the airport. He told me they had told the media no—I had experienced enough; just leave me alone. This disappointed me because I wanted to be on TV. Everyone loves to be on TV or in the newspaper; I figured I'd never have that chance again . . . boy was I wrong.

The only thing I remember about LAX was walking down this extremely long hallway to get to the gate. I boarded the plane and got a window seat. This was my first ride on an airplane, and I was pumped up. I sat with my nose pressed to the window, waiting for takeoff. I could see the other planes taking off, and it looked so cool.

As our plane took off, I could see the lights of the city below. It was beautiful. Then as the plane started to turn, the lights turned to darkness. I could see nothing out my window. The other side of the plane was getting to see all the lights. I sat up, trying to see, but I couldn't. I had hoped for a window seat, which I had gotten, but I had the window facing the Pacific Ocean. Being somewhat disappointed, I accepted a pillow from the flight attendant and went to sleep.

I woke up as the plane began its descent into New Orleans. I could see the swamps and the interstate, and I knew I was almost home. We landed, and I began walking off the plane. A couple Asian families were walking in front of me. As I walked down the ramp, I saw my mother. I got about ten feet from her, stopped, and pointed at my hair before she recognized me. She thought I was just another Asian family member.

She ran up and hugged me. As I turned around, I saw John Pastorek, a local reporter, and a news camera. After a long flight from Los Angeles and the events of the last two days, I wasn't in the mood for the news camera. I (to put it nicely) was pissed.

I asked my mother, "What are they doing here?"

She said, "Your dad called them. Now smile and act like you're happy to see us."

I was glad to be home, but I was not happy. Then came the question from John, "What do you think about all this?"

I let out a carefully rehearsed statement. I smoothly stated, "I don't know."

They filmed us walking through the airport like such a happy family, but at the time we weren't. Uncle Robert was there along with Bubba. Bubba got a few seconds of airtime when the news played that night. They showed a shot of him looking out the airport window, anxiously awaiting his little brother's return. That was what it looked like, but he told me he was looking at all the airplanes.

We then got in Robert's car and headed straight to Robert's favorite restaurant, McDonald's. As Robert saw the Golden Arches, he said, "Ronald, I knew you wouldn't let me down." After eating my first "real meal" (if you want to call it that) in two days, we drove an hour to Baton Rouge. *Home at last!*

CHAPTER 8:

Welcome Back

When I arrived home, there was what felt like one thousand people over at our house. My first concern was getting some sleep, and my mother's concern was over my hair. She hated it black and wanted it back to blond as soon as possible. Before that would happen, though, I had to go to the Baton Rouge Police Department to answer some more questions.

We went to Mike Barnett's office, where I finally got to meet him. I wasn't too thrilled to be there, and I gave the cold shoulder in response to anything anyone said to me. Mike Barnett tried to lighten the mood by cracking a joke, and I didn't even laugh. I didn't even try to fake it; I didn't think it was funny. My mother got pissed off, and I heard all about it later.

Two policemen, Captain Bueto and Captain Ryals, took me into another room for questioning that went on for about two hours. They started out in a positive mood, and they were nice, and I gave them details about what Jeff and I did on the trip. They listened to the stories; I told them about how I'd seen the house where *The Munsters* had been filmed, which was located across the street from the bus station in Orange, Texas. Later I found out that was not the truth . . . that was just what Jeff had lied and told me. (I didn't find this out till I was much older.) I told them about how we saw a bum who peed in the street and how he told us we were standing in it, the nutty guy preaching at the park, and the whore at the bus stop. They were deeply interested in my story. I was having fun talking while they took notes.

Then came, "Now, we'd like to ask you a few things that you may have left out . . ."

"Did Jeff molest you?"

"Did Jeff touch you?"

There were many more questions along these lines. Basically the same song and dance I'd faced with the questioning in California, except one thing was different . . . these guys got mean.

They started raising their voices. They tried to threaten me. They tried to trick me. Everything. These guys were vicious. They had me scared to death, but I kept my cool. I stuck to my story, didn't change one thing, and continued to lie.

People wonder why I was still lying. They can't figure out why I was still protecting Jeff. First of all, I wasn't protecting Jeff—I was protecting me. I knew if I told on Jeff, someone would tell Jeff what I had done. I figured he would get out of jail and come to me, mad, asking why I'd told. Which he would have.

I also couldn't forget Dr. Jelly-Finger and the two cotton swabs. (Sounds like the name of a rock group or something.) I knew it was a matter of time before the hospital came back with 100 percent proof I was lying. The hospital was going to be the one to tell on Jeff and get him in trouble, not me.

Finally, the two police officers gave in. They went back and talked to my parents. They told them, "What we just put that kid through was hell. Two things—either that man never fooled with that boy, because he would have cracked, or he is so brainwashed he will never admit it."

After we got home, Mom went to work on my hair. Big mistake. If you have ever experimented with hair dyes, then you know black to blond is a bitch. First it turned orange. I looked like Annie Lennox when she was with the Eurythmics. I went around the neighborhood, singing, "Sweet dreams are made of this . . ."

Then came purple, then green, and then came a yellow, almost-glowing orange—yellow-brick-road-ish gold. It was horrible, but it was what I had to live with until my hair grew out. My hair was so ugly that it glowed in the dark. If you don't believe me, put this book down, dye your hair black, and then try to dye it blond.

See!

I spent the weekend being welcomed back by my family and friends. I also spent time reading the articles in the paper about me. I had made the Shreveport newspaper. I was famous.

I got mad at a few things that I read in the articles. One, they said I thought it was a game, a vacation. I knew it wasn't a vacation, and I definitely didn't think it was a game—that made me sound stupid. Second, they said I was twelve, when I was eleven. I had always thought the real newspaper was accurate and the *Star* and the *National Enquirer* were the ones that stretched the truth, but certainly not in this case.

As Monday rolled around, I was set to return to school. I thought, "No big deal; nobody there knows. They don't read the paper. The only thing I have to do is explain my hair." *Wrong.*

As I entered the gym, I saw my friend Brian sitting across the basketball court on the stage with about six girls around him. I slowly walked toward them. I hadn't walked ten feet when I realized everyone in the gym was quiet. I looked around, but I couldn't find E. F. Hutton. (You may recall the old commercial that said, "When E. F. Hutton talks, people listen.") That's when I noticed all the people looking at me. The whole school watched me walk across the gym and didn't say anything. Most of the people knew what had happened, but others stayed quiet and stared because everyone else was.

As I got close to Brian and the girls, I could see the tears garnering in the girls' eyes. They all sat speechless as I looked at them. They had all agreed before I'd gotten there to act like nothing had happened, but something gave it away. I knew they were uncomfortable. It was up to me to ease the tension.

I calmly asked them, "What are y'all looking at? Y'all are acting like I've been kidnapped or something."

Some of the girls busted out crying, others hugged me, and Brian laughed his ass off. They welcomed me back, gave me hugs, and told me how glad they were to see me. And all this time I'd never known they really liked me.

When I went into my first class, there was a big banner that said, "Welcome back, Jody!" The whole class had signed it and put little notes on it. They had my picture and signature up on the bulletin board. The class felt just as uncomfortable as my reunion with my friends, so I again decided to take it upon myself to ease the tension.

I noticed my picture was next to an article that read, "Boy in Plastic Bubble Dies." I told them, "Y'all didn't give me much of a chance, did y'all?" as I pointed to the picture and the article. Some people laughed; some cried. It was very nice to know that everyone really cared about me, especially Christy Lucas.

Christy was the girl I had sat next to all year. Every day I used to talk with her and the smartest girl in class, Susan Roland. Christy was the one who had to put up with me every day. And surprisingly, she was one of the ones most excited about my return.

Brian Vandegrift was my best friend, and he sat on the other side of me, opposite of Christy. I used to tell Brian jokes every day at school, making him laugh and getting him in trouble. Brian was very smart and always made good grades. Thanks to that, so did I.

The whole time I had been in school while Jeff was molesting me, I'd had six As and one B in reading. School had been my escape. When I returned to school now, everything was different. I had no worries. I could be myself. I loved school and the friends I had then. I often wonder how everyone is doing. Thanks to modern-day technology, I have connected with many of my friends from back then through Facebook.

The entire day was spent with me answering questions about what had happened. Even the students wanted to know if Jeff had fooled with me. I just told them, "Hey, he took me to Disneyland," and I showed them the ticket stub. Some made the comment that they wished he would have taken them, but I never told them the cost of admission. They were too young; they wouldn't have understood.

Only once did I ever have anyone say anything real derogatory to me. This one guy (I remember his name, but I'm not going to reveal it) said to me in front of the whole PE class, "At least Jeff Doucet didn't fuck me up the ass."

Boy, was that a mistake. I let it slide. I figured he should be glad that was true. You can say what you want about me—that shit doesn't bother me.

But it bothered the other kids in the class. It wasn't like he had revealed top secret information; everybody knew, and I think most of their parents had explained the situation, but they felt that the comment was a little unnecessary. They had a mob ready to lynch this guy on the bus ride home. When the bus stopped, he knew he was getting his ass whupped, but he ran like a rabbit hound, and nobody could catch him.

The next day we were called to the office, and everything was settled. I told them it didn't bother me; it was the other kids who were bothered.

Then came March 8. Mom told me Mike Barnett wanted to talk to her the next day, and she couldn't figure out why. I knew it was time for the report to be in, but I didn't say anything.

The next day at school, I was nervous. I didn't want the final bell to ring. I knew it was time for the truth. I briefly considered making up a story about some guy who had gotten me at the hotel we stayed at, but I figured, "They are not that stupid. They believed the other lie, but not that one." So to save myself any trouble, I decided to tell the truth if necessary.

Mike Barnett came over to the house around noon on March 9, 1984. He sat my parents down and showed them the hospital report. It was positive. It said there was sperm in the rectum. Jeff had been raping their eleven-year-old son. I think my parents and everybody else thought it had only happened on the trip to California. But I was soon about to tell them about the past year. Daddy's reaction was to say Jeff was a dead motherfucker. Mom asked, "Mike, can you kill him?" It is easy to conclude my parents couldn't have cared less if Jeff took another breath. Both my mom and dad, as well as Mike Barnett, were crying, but Daddy kept insisting Jeff was going to die.

Part of the reason for my parents' reactions for wanting Jeff dead was because of the violation of trust he had demonstrated through grooming the whole family, not just me. They had trusted this man with not just me, but with my two brothers and other young boys. They had welcomed him into their home and given him clothes. They had fed him and let him stay over, and all the while he was having sex with me behind their backs. Many parents feel this way when such a violation of trust takes place.

Mike took their reactions as normal, considering what they had just found out. He knew they were both distraught, he knew they'd had very little sleep, if any, in the past three weeks, and he knew Mom had lost fifteen pounds from not eating. Considering both of their states of mind, this was the normal reaction.

Sure enough, I had known that was why Mike Barnett wanted to meet with my parents. Mom was waiting at the bus stop for us. She told me, and only me, to get in the car. She drove me home and sat me on the couch. She told me, "Mike Barnett came over today, and the hospital report came back positive."

Trying for my last-ditch effort of stupidity, I said, "What does that mean?"

She said, "That means Jeff fooled with you."

"He did," was the next thing out of my mouth. The feeling I got was incredible. Finally . . . the truth! It felt like the weight of the world was lifted off my back.

After our conversation, I left the house, went down the street, and for the first time in over a year, I joined Bubba and the girls of the neighborhood. They were at Crystal Caldwell's house, the other neighborhood hangout besides my house. That was where the girls were at.

As I approached, I saw them sitting in the ditch. I got off the bike I was riding, jumped in the ditch with them, and was finally able to be myself outside of school without worrying about getting in trouble. Let me tell you—if you have a hard time understanding how good that felt, be glad because you haven't had an experience like mine.

School and everything else was seeming to get back to normal. There was no more questioning by the police. There was no need; they knew the truth and had the proof. When Thursday, March 15, rolled around,

I got to tell the whole class about the scene on *Hill Street Blues* that was airing that night. It was the one we had watched being filmed.

That night, the family got together and watched the show. After, my dad stayed around to watch the LSU vs. Dayton basketball game. Dayton beat LSU in the first round of the NCAA tournament that year. After the game, I remember my mother staying out, talking to my father for a long time.

Up to this point, my father and I had not discussed the molesting. I told Mom not to tell him any details. I was upset to find out he knew. Mom told me he was my father, and he deserved to know. She told me Mike Barnett had told him at the same time that he'd told her. But she told me she wouldn't tell him anything else I had told her.

When my mother came in, I asked her what she had been doing. She said they'd been talking. I asked her if she'd told him anything, and she said no. Later, I found out she had been trying to get the .38-caliber snub-nosed gun my father had taken from the top of the closet. He was armed and dangerous.

CHAPTER 9:

Flight 595

Thursday, March 15, Major Mike Barnett and Lieutenant Bud Connor flew to California to extradite Jeff back to Baton Rouge. Mike had told Mom but didn't tell Daddy. Mike had told her not to tell him. She didn't. She knew Jeff would be coming in at nine thirty on Friday evening. The reason they didn't want Daddy to know was because he was still insisting on killing Jeff. Plus, he had the gun. Mike Barnett told my mother, "Relax; I have been protecting prisoners long before Gary decided to become an assassin."

Mike and Bud picked up Jeff around noon that Friday. Bud and Jeff rode in the back of the car with John O'Neill, an agent with the Santa Ana division of the FBI. Mike followed. As Bud and Jeff sat in the car on the way to the airport, Jeff asked Bud if he was Catholic. Bud said he was. Jeff then said he had something he wanted to confess to because he wanted "absolution." Bud said he was not a priest but would listen to what he had to say.

Jeff stated he had not eaten in seventeen days and planned on fasting for at least thirty more. Then he told the history of his childhood. He confessed to molesting me. Bud asked if I was the only one, and Jeff said yes. Bud said he did not believe him but would continue to listen. This was about the time they arrived at the airport. Jeff told Agent O'Neill he would call him and tell him the story once he arrived in Baton Rouge. Agent O'Neill told Jeff to call anytime. Mike and Bud then escorted Jeff through the Los Angeles airport, boarding flight 595—final destination, Baton Rouge.

Once on the plane, Jeff began an emotional confession. At many points, they would have to give him time to gain his composure because he was crying so heavily, something he was good at. And I do mean *good*. He told about his relationship with me and two other kids. I know for a fact that he had relationships with the other kids, but the facts he gave about them were questionable. For instance, he claimed that over the course of a year, he'd molested me on ten occasions. Mostly engaging in oral sex, with him performing it on me.

He then stated that he'd told me not to tell because if I did, he would go to jail. This was a complete lie. He never told me not to tell; I just didn't. Then the lies got bigger. To me, they are funny. For some odd reason, I find much humor in his reasoning and his explanations. Jeff told Bud Connor that he'd told me, "If you tell on me, the guys in prison will do to me what I am doing to you—the niggers." (Yes, besides being a pedophile, Jeff was also racist.) "That would not be right," he claimed to have said, "because what we are doing is special, and what they would do would be unnatural." He also claimed that he told me if I wanted him to stop, he would. The reason he hadn't stopped, supposedly, was because I had insisted upon it and because we loved each other and enjoyed being close to each other.

I must take a moment and comment. First, he never told me he would stop and never told me not to tell, and I never insisted on it. Give me a fucking break. An eleven-year-old asking a twenty-five-year-old to suck his dick, then to screw him up the ass? What he did say to me was that if people found out, he would go to jail, and the inmates ("niggers") would do it to him, and that would not be right.

There was also a point in my life when I wished dreadful things on Jeff, when I thought that him getting it up the ass would be good for him. I wished (this is sick but true) I was old enough to shoot off so I could cum in his mouth. The only bad thing about that was he probably would have enjoyed it. Now, years later, I have different thoughts about that. When I first started working at the Victim Services Center of Montgomery County in 1998, my then coworker Emily Greytak explained to me that rape is rape, and if you're against it, you're against it. I now don't wish that on any prisoner or anyone. There is a movement to stop prisoner rape, which I fully support, called PREA: Prison Rape Elimination Act (passed in 2003 with unanimous support from both parties in Congress).

Don't get confused with me taking out my frustration, and don't think this is how I feel now. I cared about Jeff. I shamefully admit that. Like any two people care for each other. But when he was molesting me, I hated him. When he was molesting me, these vengeful wishes were the thoughts that were in my mind. I have often said that if Jeff hadn't molested children, he would have been a kid's dream. He played with us, did fun things with us, took us to the movies, and bought us gifts. But I also know that the only reason he did this was to molest us.

I know a guy right now who has had serious problems because of Jeff. I feel it is because he is ashamed that he loved a grown man. But (and I say this directly to you, and you know who you are) there is nothing to be ashamed of. You were manipulated and brainwashed.

Children need nurturing. That is a natural need for any child along with looking up to older people whom they emulate. Sex offenders misdirect those needs to satisfy their own sexual desires. And by sexualizing a child early, they confuse the child's lovemap. The child misinterprets his or her feelings as relationship love when they really are not yet mature enough to really feel those feelings. Then, as a child grows into an adult, they *can't* unlearn what they know now as an adult, and they look back on what they felt with their new adult consciousness. So they think they should have known. But that really wasn't possible.

You were conditioned to love him. It was a carefully thought-out plan, done over and over to kids, more than just you and me. Any kid Jeff picked would have fallen in love . . . we were young and didn't understand why we felt that way. That was his security. That way, he knew you wouldn't tell. Through countless guilt trips and crying to you, making you feel sorry because he had no one. Hell, he could have had someone if he would have quit fucking children.

It's time you leave the past in the past. Accept what happened as a part of life, and move on. Use your knowledge and experience as something learned, and keep it from happening to your kid or any other kid. It's okay that you felt the way you did. You were a kid—a baby. You're an adult now. You still have people who love and care for you. I talked to your dad before he died; he loved you. His only hope in the world was for your well-being. The same as my dad. The only difference is that my dad went about it a different way. Now, think about what you want out of life. Get your dreams off the ground, keep the faith, and get yourself straight and back on the right track.

The problems that seem to follow you around are not the true problem. They are symptoms of the problem. They are signs. Talk about it. Hell, it's been long enough—get it out. Then you, too, will see what it is like to get the weight of the world lifted off your shoulders. Seek help; hopefully you can move forward, and everything will be okay.

It is not like I'm some stranger to your circumstances. I know. I went through the exact same thing because of the exact same man.

Jeff's confession went on throughout the whole plane trip. He stated that he wanted to talk with the three kids and their parents alone so he could advise the parents to get the kids some psychiatric help. What a "Good Samaritan" Jeff was now turning out to be.

The plane had a stop at Dallas/Fort Worth International Airport. From there, it was an hour and fifteen minutes to Baton Rouge.

Daddy spent that day in emotional turmoil. He was visiting the Cotton Club. He was sitting next to a guy named Bob Schadel. Bob was the program director for WBRZ, Channel 2, the local ABC affiliate. He asked my dad if he knew when they were bringing Jeff back. Daddy said, "No, I don't. I think they have brought him back already."

Bob then said, "He is not back yet. Wait one minute; I'll find out for you." He got up, called the station, and then told my dad, "They were scheduled to arrive at nine thirty tonight." I don't think Bob did this thinking my dad was going to do what he did. Bob was just trying to be helpful by letting my dad know when Jeff would be back in town. And when I say *helpful*, I mean by creating a news story.

Daddy then got on the phone. He was very upset. He called my mother and wanted details as to what happened to me. She was reluctant to tell him, but Daddy insisted. He kept asking, "Did he make Jody suck his dick? Did he make Jody suck his dick?" For some reason that was my dad's biggest concern. Like getting screwed wasn't enough.

My mother, with knowledge of the truth, finally told him yes, as well as other specifics. Going against my demands. My specific instructions, "Don't tell Daddy."

This information was more than he could handle. He called my grandparents and told them to pick up us kids when we got off from school. Remember, this was Friday, March 16—my dad's weekend to have us.

School was fun for me that day. The whole class watched the *Hill Street Blues* show. They thought it was so cool because they knew what was going to happen. Even Mrs. Julie Levert, my teacher, watched it and enjoyed it. She found it neat to know what was going to happen. She also thought it was neat that I had been able to see them film it.

As I got off the bus to go home that day, nothing seemed to make the day any different than the rest. My grandparents came to pick us up. I got pissed off at my dad for not being there.

We went out to our camp at False River. I tried to catch fish barehanded, took a bath, and went to bed without watching the news.

My father called a friend—Jim "Stinky" Adams—from a pay phone at Jerry's Quick Stop on False River, about two miles from the camp. Daddy told Stinky he couldn't take it anymore and was going to attempt to shoot Jeff. Stinky tried to tell my Dad otherwise, but it was too late—the phone was dead.

Stinky called the Central Police Department and talked to Sergeant Murphy. He told him about a prisoner arriving at the airport and that his friend might try to shoot him. Stinky asked for Mike Barnett's phone number. Sergeant Murphy was not authorized to give it out, but he said he would try to get in touch with Barnett, and he would give Mike Stinky's number.

Daddy arrived at the airport around nine o'clock that evening. He walked right up the stairs at the Baton Rouge Metropolitan Airport and got on a pay phone. At the time, in 1984, there was a row of twelve phones at the Baton Rouge Metropolitan Airport located right before you get to the metal detectors. To exit the airport, you must go down the escalator or the stairs, passing right in front of the phones.

He also got on the phone located across from TV cameraman Abram McGull. Daddy knew that if the camera was there, Jeff, Mike Barnett, and Bud Connor would probably walk by. Daddy had on a white Riverland Equipment hat, along with dark sunglasses. He had on a pair of blue jeans, a purple-and-white horizontal-striped shirt, and cowboy boots with a .38-caliber snub-nosed revolver stuck securely in them.

He was talking on the phone again to Jim "Stinky" Adams. He told Stinky he was at the airport and was going to shoot Jeff.

As the plane landed in Baton Rouge, Mike, Jeff, and Bud talked about the plans. Bud told Jeff to look for any of the parents of the boys he'd molested. Jeff also said he would look for his brother Sam. He said Sam was crazy and might try to break him out if he didn't know about him molesting children. He also said that if Sam did know of him molesting children, he might try to kill him too.

Bud told Jeff that if he saw anyone, he should yell and hit the floor. Bud would jump on top of Jeff, and Mike would apprehend the parent. Mike went first, looking for anyone he recognized, especially Daddy. He didn't see Daddy because his head was buried in the phone booth. Bud and Jeff saw the camera, and Bud told Jeff he should put his head down but keep an eye out.

My father told Stinky, "The news media are here. I see them coming." But when he saw Mike and not Jeff, he said, "Oh, they took him out a different way." Then the lights from the camera came on. "No, they're coming and are going to walk right past me." Daddy had his back turned to Jeff, Mike, Bud, and the news camera. He knew when the lights shined on him that they were near.

"I'm pulling the gun out of my boot. You're going to hear the shot." Then the phone went silent. Soon after, Stinky received a phone call from Sergeant Murphy telling him he couldn't reach Mike Barnett. Stinky said, "It's too late. I just talked with Gary. I heard the shot; then the phone went dead."

Jeff and Bud received the signal from Mike to proceed. Jeff walked arrogantly, first looking at the camera, then turning his head, looking straight forward. He licked his lips, took about sixteen steps, and dropped. The force from the bullet broke his neck as he fell into the fetal position on the floor.

Bud Connor dropped to one knee, reaching for his gun. Mike Barnett said, "Whoa, God damnit! Gary, why? Why, Gary?" as he lunged for my dad, shielding him from Bud. Mike grabbed my dad's arm and held it straight in the air as Bud walked over and took the gun. Bud made sure Mike had everything under control, called my dad a son of a bitch, and walked over to Jeff. He said, "Goddamn" as he shook his head and knelt next to Jeff's lifeless body.

Bud shook his head, then closed Jeff's eyes.

Bud got up and identified himself as a sheriff's deputy, asking someone to call 9-1-1. He turned toward my dad and asked him, "Why in the fuck would you do that?"

Daddy looked at him, crying, and said, "If he would have done that to your family, you would have done the same thing too . . . you don't know. You know what he did to Jody. Any father would have done it. I had to do it."

Abram McGull—the cameraman, who later became a resident legal adviser at the US Department of State—got it all on camera. Everything. He didn't miss a thing. He was steady as can be, or as steady as one could be under such circumstances. I believe he would win awards for this footage. As a matter of fact, about a minute and five seconds after McGull started filming, while the police were responding to the chaos, he quietly changed the tape in case police tried to seize what he had recorded as evidence. He recognized immediately that he had recorded something extraordinary.

At the time, it was one of the few murders recorded on film. Thanks to YouTube, the video of the shooting has over twenty million views and seems to pop up on my Facebook page every other week.

Abram McGull would later respond to me when I messaged him on Facebook regarding that night. He said, "It was a chaotic night, but many understood what your father did that night." In regard to the title *Why, Gary, Why?* he said, "The title of the book emphasizes what was on every parent's heart once they knew the full story. I will never forget your father's compassionate and loving answer to that question. At that moment, there was a raw understanding of a wrong being right."

However, in an article published in the *Springfield News-Leader* in 2018, McGull would say, "I am opposed to vigilante justice. The Sixth Amendment of our Constitution says every accused is entitled to a speedy and public trial. That's important."

McGull said there's a lot of value in a public trial so the community can see that people who commit crimes are held accountable for their actions.

Furthermore, McGull said prosecutors do not like turning sympathetic crime victims into defendants.

And I agree with him 100 percent. Despite the terrible things Jeff had done, as an American citizen, he had a right to a trial. Hell, his brother Roland went to Vietnam to fight for those rights.

After securing my father and putting him in handcuffs, Mike said, "Book him—second-degree murder," thankfully taking first-degree murder off the table, because to the untrained eye, it could have looked premeditated. But I can promise you, knowing my dad, he had put little planning into it. Had he thought about it too much, he would have failed.

My mother arrived home from her sister Honey's house about five minutes to ten o'clock. She turned on the TV. As she walked across the living room, she heard Jay Young the local anchorman. She was planning on watching Jeff's return from California.

When she heard the news brief saying, "Unknown assailant guns down alleged kidnapper at the Baton Rouge Airport; details at ten," her legs went out. She started screaming and crying. She tried viciously with all her might to get up and get to a phone, but her legs were paralyzed. She couldn't walk. Shaking, screaming, and crying, she repeatedly said, "No, no, no."

The neighbors heard the screaming and rushed over, arriving at the same time the police did. They tried to calm her down, but it was no use. She was hysterical.

The footage was shown on the news that night and every night after that for what seemed like a year. It was instant headlines. CNN, CBS, ABC, NBC, the *Washington Post*, the *New York Times*. It seemed like everyone was covering the story.

That next day—Saturday, March 17—my grandparents woke my siblings and me up and drove us back to Baton Rouge. We kept asking, "Where's Daddy?" I figured he'd gotten a DWI or something.

When we arrived, we played for a minute. Then we saw my mother drive up with Uncle Robert. I figured Daddy had been killed in a car wreck or something. My mother sat us four kids on the steps and told us why our dad hadn't made it to the river. I couldn't believe what I heard.

My mother said, "Last night, Daddy shot Jeff."

Bubba was not even phased. He could not have cared one way or the other.

Mikey said, "Good."

Sissy started to cry, saying, "My daddy's going to jail."

My reaction was by far the most dramatic. I started crying, mad at what Daddy had done. I hated Jeff and yet felt I loved Jeff. I, at the time, had only wished that Jeff would stop molesting me. If he wasn't molesting kids, he was great. I know I keep saying that, but that was what I thought. This is a classic example of the ambivalent feelings that develop when a child is taken advantage of sexually by a man or woman they look up to, admire, and want to emulate.

I did not wish him dead. But now, I had just been told he was on life support, waiting to die, being kept alive only to donate his organs. I went to the side of my grandparents' house and cussed at my mother. I was crying heavily, and she tried to comfort me.

I was pissed, mad, hurt, disappointed, and confused. Everyone kept telling me that Daddy killed Jeff for me—if that was true, shouldn't he have asked me first? I didn't want him dead; Dad did, meaning he killed him for himself and only himself.

We went back to our house, and a ton of people were over. It was very chaotic. Everyone was telling me how much my father loved me and that he only did it for me. This was not what I wanted to hear. It was not for me; it was for him, and nobody could tell me otherwise.

I was instructed not to watch the news or look at the paper. Yeah, right. I walked to the Village Pharmacy, located directly behind my house, just out our back gate. I saw James, the owner, and he told me he'd seen the news and that he wished my family the best. Then I walked to the Village Grocery, which was a block away, to get a Snickers candy bar. I remember being very light headed, almost in a dream state. Then I got upset. I sat down behind the six-foot back fence to our backyard, thought about the last year, and cried.

After crying for about an hour, all by myself, hiding in the backyard, I joined the commotion. Bubba was looking for me. He was ready to break the joint and get the fuck out of there. He was going to Shay

Johnson's house to ride the gigantic rope swing in his backyard, and he wanted to know if I wanted to come.

Almost like a robot, I said, "Sure, why not?" We rode to Shay's, where a few other kids had decided to take turns on the swing. I sat and watched at first. Shay had a newspaper, so, doing as I had been told not to, I looked at it. It wasn't as bad as the grown-ups thought it would be. I was somewhat comforted by the pictures. They made me feel better.

Okay. Enough of the shooting—it was time to swing. The swing was a blast. If there still was a swing like that today, I would go ride it. It was the perfect distraction to keep my mind off reality. When it was time to go home, most of my thoughts were about getting back on the swing.

That night, I watched the news. I became fascinated with the whole thing. I watched the footage of the shooting over and over on VHS. I used to watch it so much I would get in trouble. I would reenact it in the living room, the mall, everywhere. I argued over how close my dad was. Mom said about ten feet. I said a foot, maybe.

We were flying to Dallas a couple of months later, my first time back to the airport in Baton Rouge. When I got there, I studied the scene. The phone, the spot he fell, and the path they walked. It was so peaceful. There was no bloodstain, no sign of murder, nothing. It was so strange.

Meanwhile, the news media kept wanting to hear our side of the story. The Doucets had already made the claim that it was a crime of passion, that my father shot Jeff because he was upset because Jeff took his wife from him. Roland, Jeff's closest brother, was the family spokesman.

According to Jeff's confession on the plane ride home, he'd told Roland about molesting me. My mother had talked to Roland the night before the shooting and had told him about the hospital report, so Roland knew the truth. But also—in defense of Roland for the claims he was making—to him, the truth also was that my mother and Jeff had a relationship. That is what Jeff had told him for the past nine months, so it was only fitting Roland believed this.

Roland never really faced the issue of me; he always brought up the issue of my mother. He has never denied Jeff molested me, but he has never confirmed it either. He has evaded the issue. His biggest and most understandable claim he made was that Jeff deserved his day in court.

With the allegations of Jeff and my mother's relationship, the people of Baton Rouge not knowing what to believe, and my family not standing up and defending us, my mother was losing it. Once Roland was on a radio talk show, talking about the relationship between Jeff and my mother, and she went absolutely nuts. She was crying, trying to get through on the telephone, upset and hurt because Roland knew the truth. She couldn't understand that Roland was trying to defend his family name and that in the long run, by us not talking, the truth would eventually come out.

A lot of people in Baton Rouge believe till this day that Jeff and my mother had a romantic relationship. It was more sadistic than romantic. The reason so many people believed this was, believe it or not, because of my dad. When my mother had told my father to leave in July of 1983, it had been because of his drinking. Also, when she left him again in 1991, it was because of his drinking.

Daddy, being a man with pride, not wanting to believe it was because of his drinking, started telling people it was because she was seeing Jeff. Because of the many people he knew, the word spread around town like wildfire that my mother and Jeff were a couple. So, long before Roland made this claim, the town already believed it. As soon as Roland started stressing it, people automatically believed it. That said, many child predators use the cover of a romantic relationship to gain access to a single woman's children. This is why online dating sites where women mention in their profiles, "Proud mother of two beautiful young girls" concern me because it makes it easy for predators to find their prey.

One day I was sitting out in the front yard when this car pulled up. This guy got out, walked to the door, and knocked. Within a minute he was back in his car, driving away. I then found out he was with the London newspaper the *Times* or some other London newspaper. I was amazed. London. People in London had heard about the story. The reporters coming by and calling on the phone got so bad that Mom decided we needed to get out of town, so we loaded up the car and drove to Biloxi to go visit Uncle Raymond, my godfather.

CHAPTER 10:

Finding Me

In Biloxi, us kids could be ourselves. Away from all the attention and away from all the distractions. We missed school for a week, but I'm sure the absences were excused.

My godmother, Lois, took us to the Keesler Air Force Base to watch a parade. Then she took us to the beach to feed the seagulls. She took us to do different and fun things we weren't used to doing. At this time, the most important thing was to keep me busy, to keep my mind off of things. This is something kids do better than adults. Kids seem to roll with the punches and go with the flow; they don't dwell on their problems as long as adults do, or at least they don't dwell on their problems until they become adults.

At Raymond's, we took pictures with my new Kodak disc camera. We shot videotapes of the kids playing in the den. It is so funny to go back there and watch the tape. We all were so young, and my hair was so fucking ugly.

When school started back up, everyone was telling me they had seen the news. So much so to the point where it seemed as though all of their comments just blended together; you couldn't separate one comment from the other, just like on *The View*.

Two important events I remember well that really signified another behavioral change for the better was going to Mississippi and riding horses with my neighbor Wayne Atkinson and going to a birthday party for a friend, Kristie Schexnayder—the same Kristie Schexnayder who had been a witness to my kidnapping.

Both the events took place on the same weekend. First, Mr. Wayne, Bubba, and I went to Mississippi. We visited Mr. Wayne's parents' house between Woodville and Centerville. Once we got there, we had our choice between three-wheelers or horses. First, we chose the three-wheelers.

For hours, or at least until the three-wheelers ran out of gas, Bubba and I rode through the woods, by the river, and across the fields. Mr. Wayne's parents had a lot of land, so we did a lot of riding. We saw rabbits and raccoons and all kinds of different animals. I remember going full blast on this little three-wheeler across the field. What I didn't know was that field used to be a garden, so it was all wavy, with uneven ground. As I hit the waves in the grass, the three-wheeler went flying about ten feet over my head. I landed about thirty feet from where I had taken off, only to have the baby three-wheeler land on top of me. But I was okay.

Then came the horses. This was scary because my legs weren't long enough for my feet to fit into the saddle properly. Bubba rode this little bitty horse that seemed about one hundred and fifty years old. This horse was so old, the glue factory had sent it back.

Once I mounted my horse (this was the first time I ever rode a horse), it took off. I was holding on for dear life. Bubba's horse could barely walk. I think Betty White was given that horse for her fifth birthday, so if it was going to move more than two feet, this horse was bound to faint.

Meanwhile, Secretariat—or at least he ran like Secretariat—was still running like the dog in *Funny Farm*. The horse was fast. I was scared to death and was thrilled once I got off. The only other time I was that scared was the first time I rode with Mikey in a car. He was going so fast that he passed Jeff Gordon and Chuck Yeager. I think Mikey was the first man to break the sound barrier in a 1978 Ford Fiesta.

We ate dinner in Mississippi, then headed home. Mr. Wayne's mama cooked the best cornbread I have ever eaten. I felt like a pig eating as much as I did, but it was only a compliment to the cooking.

Right before we arrived home that night, we stopped by McDonald's for ice cream. What Mr. Wayne then experienced was Jody turning back into Jody. As the lady handed me my ice cream, I immediately stuck the ice cream to my forehead. Mr. Wayne hadn't been ready for that, but he laughed. He thought it was hilarious.

The next night was Kristie's party. It wasn't the first party I had been invited to, but it was the first one I went to because before, Jeff wouldn't have let me go. Hell, I threw the invitations away so he wouldn't see it. God forbid I should have fun at school without him. Jeff being able to control me even when he was not around is an example of *coercive control*. It's a level higher than grooming and is much more controlling.

My best friend, Brian, was there with a black eye. He'd been hit by a pitch to the eye. Way to keep an eye on the ball, Brian. He was after these girls, I was acting a fool, and Bubba was watching us, laughing.

I was a force of uninhibited energy, completely out of control. Brian, on the other hand, was trying to spray his territory like a tomcat on the prowl. Brian had no luck while we were there, but we left early. Then Monday at school, to my and Bubba's disbelief, Brian told us he'd made out with the one girl he'd been after. We were shocked.

After the party, I felt comfortable around my peers. They get the credit for it because obviously, they understood. They did all they could to make me feel comfortable and accepted.

Being me at this time really wasn't that bad. If you can believe it, I was popular, everyone said hey, and everyone talked to me, even Monique Saint Clergy, the prettiest girl in school. I made new friends and was more active and sociable around school. Then the inevitable happened. I discovered "the phone."

I had made friends with Cary Jones, one of the tallest and prettiest girls in school, and we used to talk for hours. I also started to call and talk to Christy. Cary and Christy both eventually came to like me, but I liked Christy as more than a friend. I wanted to "go" with Christy. Christy would later go on to become my first official girlfriend. Once, though, in first grade, I did get married to a beautiful blonde named Missy Simmons in a ceremony performed by me in the back of the class.

With all my new friends and my twelfth birthday coming up, I decided to have a party. It was a blast. We had a ton a people come over. I had a wonderful time, and I hope everyone who came enjoyed themselves too.

School was now coming to an end. I remember an eclipse that year and the space shuttle flying over Baton Rouge en route to the world's fair in New Orleans. I also remember a teary-eyed Christy asking me to come to the last day of school. I was exempt from my last two exams and didn't plan on going, but then Christy, who had a locker right next to mine, asked me so sincerely to "please come tomorrow." Being cold-hearted, as I would later become to Christy in the worst way, I didn't go.

I did keep in touch with her and Cary over the summer. Christy even introduced me to her best friend and neighbor, Katy McDougal. Yes, that is her real name. I split my time on the phone between Christy, Cary, and Katy. I called Katy to find out if Christy liked me.

Meanwhile, Bubba, Brian, and I hung out all summer together. Once, I had Brian call Christy and ask her if she liked me. We taped the conversation because our cordless phone played over the radio.

The first time I really discussed anything about Jeff with anybody other than my mother was with Christy and Cary. I knew Brian knew, and we joked about it occasionally, but Christy and Cary weren't sure. I remember getting choked up as I told them, almost starting to cry. This was because I felt really close to Christy and Cary. I could trust them.

Like I said earlier, Brian and I did everything together. At least until we went to different high schools. But even today, we are still best friends. Brian and I used to stay up late, talking about the future and trying to stay up all night. The first night we accomplished our goal was on my mother's birthday: August 16, 1985.

We would make a big pot of coffee and drink it to keep us awake. We would try to make it to see *Kids Incorporated* air the next morning because I was in love with Gloria (Martika). After that, we would sleep the rest of the day.

Brian came with us to the Saints football games, to the Woodlawn football games, and anywhere else I went. We often played football, basketball, and baseball together. We would swim in his pool and try to get in trouble. But we never did.

At the National Beta Club Convention, we would chase the girls all night. I would never succeed; I have never been good with the women I wanted. But Brian was smooth. He had tons of girlfriends, but that never came between us. I was first; his girls were second.

Whenever Brian and I get together today, it's the same thing. I cut up and make him laugh. That was something Brian was good at—laughing at my dumb ass. I don't know what it is, but I could make Bubba and Brian laugh at their own funerals.

My other friends from middle school are treasures to me. They were very considerate of my situation and gave me no special treatment. They acted as though nothing had ever happened, even though they knew it had. My teacher, Mrs. Levert, is also someone very special. I could call her up just to talk if I wanted to. I would talk LSU football, baseball, and basketball with her.

I have always loved and been close to my teachers. My third-grade teacher, Mrs. Yvonne Fuller, I also called on the phone. I know I could still call them today, just to talk.

In seventh grade, I had one friend take it upon himself to do something very special for me. From 1984 to 1985, my love for LSU basketball was at an all-time high. This one friend just so happened to be a ball boy for the LSU basketball team because his dad worked in the athletic department. I was envious of his good fortune and wished I could be a ball boy for LSU's basketball team.

One day, he came to me and handed me a program from the previous night's game against Mississippi State. On the cover was assistant coach Ron Abernathy, and he had signed it, "To Jody, Best Wishes, LSU Basketball, Ron Abernathy." To say I was amped would be an understatement. Then my friend told me to open it up to the middle of the program, where they had the player profiles. He had gotten each player on the 1984–1985 LSU basketball team to autograph the program for me. Many of the players would be on the team the following year when they would reach the Final Four in Dallas.

To this day, I still have that program in mint condition, and it is one of my most prized collectables. I don't know if my friend who gave it to me, Derrick "DMac" Mallet, knows how much that meant to me, but for a kid who had experienced what I had gone through, that meant the world. It helped me gain the confidence to move forward and gave me the hope that anything was possible.

I can't list every person I would like to individually, but you know who you are. Later, when I talk about influences, I will mention more people, but for now I just want my friends to know how much they meant and still mean to me.

Your friends are the most special people one can have, and I love all my friends and all of the people who have ever influenced my life in any way. To my friends, I thank you.

CHAPTER 11:

The Justice System

My dad was taken to jail the night that he shot Jeff. He spent the weekend there. He got along great with the officers and the prisoners. There was this one prisoner whose crimes were unknown by my dad, and nobody would tell him. After the guy left, the officers told my dad the other prisoner was in because of molesting a child.

One night, this other prisoner was complaining about not having enough to eat. My dad said, "Don't worry; I'll take care of you." He then took off his boots and made a person-like figure in the bed. When the officers handed out food, my dad said, "Shorty . . . wake up. Wake up, Shorty."

He told the officers Shorty was really tired and that they should just leave him a plate, and he would eat it later. He then gave the extra plate to the guy who had been complaining.

Daddy's bail was set at one hundred thousand dollars. It was posted first thing Monday morning, and he was released. At first, he went to stay with a friend, Budgie Wall. We went to visit him at Budgie's. I was real tired and fell asleep on Budgie's polar-bear rug. This bothered Daddy because he felt I was avoiding him and that I was mad at him, which, at the time, was true.

He was then admitted for psychiatric evaluation to Parkland Hospital. We visited him every weekend. The first weekend there was the first time I felt comfortable in front of him. Like me, he was changing too. He had shaved his beard, and for the first time in I don't know how long, his spirits were high.

He wasn't depressed or shaking, and he was sober. He looked great. He was also funnier than hell, which is thankfully something that came from being sober. I was feeling more relaxed with our distant relationship, but I still hadn't accepted what he had done.

Then, a couple weeks later, he was released on a weekend pass. He was real quiet and reserved. When I found out he would be staying the weekend in our home, I was nervous and avoided him.

After that came his release, and then he moved back home. He started painting, changing the tiles, adding ceiling fans, and trying to better the house we lived in. He also started to make us go to bed earlier than we were used to. This pissed me off. Who was he? He hadn't lived here in months, and now he was trying to tell us what to do?

Mom was understanding and really began enjoying my father for the first time in years. Mainly because he wasn't drinking. Dr. Ozie, my father's psychiatrist, told my mother that Daddy would never drink again, that he needed her now more than ever. She replied, "If he never drinks again, I have no problems with him."

My parents got along great, but I was still uneasy. Then—after Daddy had been home a couple months and was pretty much letting me be—my mother had a talk with me. By this time, I was relaxing and getting back to normal, so I listened. She explained that he would never drink again, that she was happy with him, and that he was my father.

After that conversation I started to heal our relationship. He let the process take care of itself. I had always been Daddy's boy, and he was glad I was coming around. The funny thing is, he never did anything to me to make me hate him. It was Jeff. Jeff made me hate him. If I had talked with Daddy or had ridden with him to the store when he'd had us for the weekend, Mikey usually would tell Jeff. Not to get me in trouble, but because Jeff would ask, and Mikey would tell. After that, here would come the guilt trip. I would get yelled at, cussed at—you name it. So as a protective device, I built a wall between me and Daddy. When he killed Jeff, I built another one. This was another perfect example of coercive control.

As the Berlin Wall eventually collapsed, so did my wall. I remember walking to the swimming pool that summer and telling my dad I didn't blame him for what he had done and that I understood. He didn't say anything, but I knew it meant a lot to him.

My dad's first lawyer was a friend of his (at least, we thought so): A. Foster Sanders, a.k.a. "Foxy." Foxy decided to defend Daddy pro bono (for free), but my dad was going to pay a high price.

Foxy supposedly set up a deal with a book publisher and a movie-production company, in which he committed that my dad's case would go to trial. A trial would generate more public interest and make for more sales of books and movie tickets, while my family would spend even more time in the public spotlight. When the news of the deal got out, so did Foxy. My dad fired his ass and hired Anthony Marabella.

Before my dad fired Foxy, I had an interview with him. In the interview, I remember Foxy asking me if I thought I was going to "grow up and be queer or molest children." How would you feel? Well, that's how I felt. I wanted to beat the shit out of Foxy. Better yet, I wanted to slap him like the bitch he was. What kind of question is that to be asking an eleven-year-old who had been molested for the past year? Give me a break.

I was pleased to learn Foxy was gone. I hold nothing against him now, but at the time I was pissed. I don't think he meant anything by it, and I believe if he had to do it over again, I would think (or at least hope) he would approach it differently. Foxy eventually ran for district attorney and lost. If he would have stayed as my father's lawyer—which he had likely planned for and was why he'd done it for free—he probably would have won. Eventually, Foxy became a judge in Baton Rouge.

Anthony approached my father's case differently. If he could find a deal worth taking, he would do it. The prosecutor, Prem Burns, was a woman, and I think that was to our benefit. At the time I didn't like her because I thought that if anyone was going to put my father in jail, it would be her. Today, I have the utmost respect for her because she's a real, heartfelt person. She prosecuted other high-profile crimes in Baton Rouge, including the hit men who took out Barry Seal and the killer of Betty Smothers. Betty Smothers was a Baton Rouge police officer and the mother of NFL great Warrick Dunn. If you don't know the good that Warrick Dunn has done in response to the tragedy of his mother being murdered, put this book down right now and google it!

I first met Prem in 1995 when we both appeared on *The Oprah Winfrey Show*. After the show, Prem, my cousin Aaron, and I went to lunch at the Omni Hotel in Chicago, where all of Oprah Winfrey's guests stayed.

A few weeks later, I found out that Prem was speaking to LSU law students. I was attending LSU at the time and went to listen to her speech. When she was finished, I said hello to her, and the student who had arranged for Prem to come speak interrupted and asked how we knew each other. I responded with, "She prosecuted my dad."

The student looked back at me, laughing, and said, "No, really—how do y'all know each other?"

Prem looked at her and said, "No, really—I prosecuted his dad!"

Back to the trial. The evidence against Jeff was enough to convict him, but Jeff was not on trial. My dad was. Hell, he was on film—there was no denying he did it. So when the time came, he entered a no-contest plea to manslaughter. The date of the sentencing was in November of 1985. Judge Frank Saia took mercy on my father. I guess the judge had kids and understood.

Judge Saia sentenced Daddy to seven years hard time.

When the Doucets heard this, they stood up and cheered. But the judge had not finished. He then suspended the sentence to five years of probation and three hundred hours of community service. The Doucets were then upset, and my family was relieved. To think of what life would have been like for my mother and us four kids if Daddy hadn't been there to support us . . . in the long run, I feel justice was served.

I do not condone taking a life or taking the law into your own hands. But I do feel everyone's life is better off with the results. My dad did his community service by working at the parish church. He mostly did maintenance around the school. He served his probation time and was a perfect citizen. From the shooting till his death, my father never had more than a traffic ticket. Okay, he had one DWI, but that's it.

Roland Doucet became a local celebrity in Baton Rouge. I feel the Doucets handled themselves in a very respectable manner. Of course, they were upset about what had happened, but the whole situation was fucked up to begin with.

I have no hard feelings for Roland or any of his family. He didn't do anything to me, and everything he said was to defend his family's name, and I understand that. I always liked Roland, and I hope he continues with what he is doing with the best of luck.

I hope the message from the case wasn't that you can "get away with murder." I hope everyone realizes it was tragic and not heroic. It's sad to think that Jeff was so messed up that he had to molest children, and it's sad to think that my dad was so messed up he had to kill someone he had once given the shirt off his back to.

It would be a mistake to think that killing someone is easy and that it is easy to live with. My father regretted that the whole situation happened, but he had felt he had to defend his family, and at the time he had felt the only way to do that was for someone to die. He told me that someone was going to die that night—either him or Jeff; it made no difference.

To think that my dad was in his right mind when he did it would be another mistake. He had been separated for nine months from his wife whom he dearly loved, and his son had been taken from him. Then he found out his son was raped. That was not your everyday, average bad news. That was more than one man could handle, or at least more than my dad could handle, and he lost it.

Remember, I had told my mother not to tell him any details. It was not until I read my dad's deposition in the civil trial that I found out what details he knew at the time of the shooting. This lawyer kept pressing my father for what details he knew about what Jeff had done to me. My dad kept it vague, saying, "Jeff molested Jody." But this lawyer wanted specifics. My dad eventually lost it, and the following are exact quotes from the deposition. This should give you an idea of why my dad was so out of his mind. The lawyer began by asking my dad what my mother had told him I'd said.

Lawyer: "What has she told you that he said?"

Daddy: "About what happened to . . ."

Lawyer: "To Jody."

Daddy: "From Jeff?"

Lawyer: "From Jeff."

Daddy: "That he used to call him his little cum-catcher—him and the other kid. And he's been fooling with him about a year. Well, two months—two or three months—after we put him in school, he started trying to fool with him. He'd put him in his lap to start out, and he'd put him in his lap to drive. And then he'd take them to movies and stuff and rub them in the movies and stuff like that, and just a bunch of gross, nasty stuff. You know. I mean I don't think details are going to help this any; do you? I mean, this is nasty, filthy shit, you know, and it makes me sick."

Lawyer: "Well, of course, to some extent the details may become relevant, and so I need to know as best you know."

Daddy: "Well, he would suck him off about every day and screw him in his butt as many times as he could a day. He hurt his back one time, and my brother-in-law went and rented a walker for him to help him, and he would prop up on the walker and get him in front of a mirror and screw him in the butt. He would do it in a McDonald's. He would do it anywhere that he could find possible to do it—in a car. He would take his shirt off and wipe his thing off with that and just throw shit rags out in the street. And he was just, you know . . . I mean, just nasty, low-down, filthy stuff, which he violated my son's rights, you know."

Lawyer: "But none of that has been told directly to you by Jody?"

Daddy: "No."

Lawyer: "Are there any medical professionals other than Dr. Brabham that Jody has seen?"

Daddy: "No."

Lawyer: "Has there been any testing done on Jody other than whatever Dr. Brabham would have done?"

Daddy: "No."

And now my favorite part. A lawyer named Mr. Iving chimed in and said, "Let's take a couple of minutes for recess here."

After they came out of the recess, a lawyer from one of the insurance companies started to ask my father questions and early on stated, "There is no reason to go into details." It reminds me of the scene in *A Time to Kill* where Samuel L. Jackson says, "Yes, they deserved to die, and I hope they burn in hell."

Finally, there were many conspiracy theories about the cops setting up Jeff, who tipped off Daddy, blah blah blah. I often hear, "If your dad did this today, he would go to jail, and he would not get off so easy." First, let me say that Daddy not only did not go to jail, but he also did not lose his job. And he had driven the company car to the airport that night.

In the 2013 ESPN *E:60*, Mike Barnett said, "They were not going to convict Gary for killing the guy who molested his son . . . not in Baton Rouge." Odds were, had Daddy gone to trial, he would have been acquitted. But why take the chance? At some point the DA was offering my father a deal with no jail time. Dr. Ozie's lawyer, Jim Boren, an excellent lawyer in Baton Rouge, had Dr. Ozie inform my father about Foxy and the TV/book deal. Dr. Ozie asked my father if he trusted him. My father said, "Yes."

Dr. Ozie said, "If I tell you something, will you do it and do it without asking me why?"

My father said, "Yes."

Dr. Ozie said, "Get rid of Foxy."

So that is what my father did—he fired Foxy. Around 2015 I stopped by a quaint, local Italian restaurant in Baton Rouge called Digiulio Brothers. John Digiulio was one of my father's lawyers and is one of the Digiulio brothers. He was having dinner with Jim Boren, and Jim Boren confirmed that story about Dr. Ozie for me. If you are ever in Baton Rouge, stop by Digiulio Brothers, and enjoy the charming atmosphere and excellent food. Also, stop by TJ Ribs and get their wings . . . sauce on the side.

CHAPTER 12:

Choices

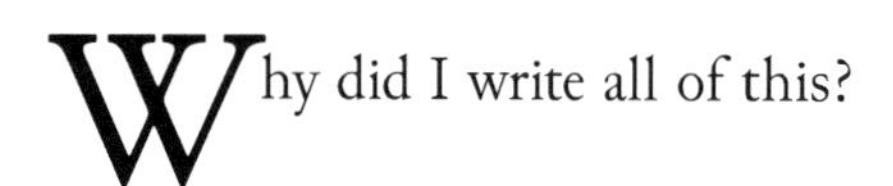

Why did I write all of this?

Why did I tell you my story?

I want you to see where you may miss the little things that could prevent or reduce the risk of this happening to your kids. There are so many things that we do that change the way kids will react in a given situation. Think about this: Do you give your kids a choice when you ask them what they want?

Consider when you take your kids out to eat, and you ask them what they want to drink, and they say, "Coke!"

Then you tell the waiter, "He'll have milk instead."

When you do this, you are conditioning the child to believe that the adult always wins. They do not have a voice even when they try. Many parents do this out of their parenting style of manipulation and control. This starts the cycle that shows the child that even when you ask them what they want, your decision and power trumps their own.

Former FBI profiler Jim Clemente likes to describe this phenomenon as children growing up in a "land of giants." He stated to me, "How can they possibly feel they have any power over adult giants . . . unless we demonstrate to them that they do in fact have that power? You were 'compliant' because he had groomed and coercively controlled you. You were ambivalent in that you loved and looked up to him but hated the victimization."

There were several red flags that had indicated Jeff had a predilection for this behavior from when I first met him up until the kidnapping.

As parents and guardians, we need to be constantly mindful of those signs. It should register as a red flag if someone wants to spend more or nearly as much time with your children as you do. Another red flag is if this adult picks out a special child.

For example, what if someone offers to have your child ride with them? What if the child doesn't want to go? Is there apprehension in his or her voice? Does he or she look scared? Is this an unusual behavior?

Don't force the child.

There may be a reason the child doesn't want to go. Is there a relative you practically have to force your kids to hug at family events and outings? Have you considered that if a child doesn't want to hug someone, it may be because he or she is uncomfortable with that person? Emotional responses can be the first signal that something is wrong. Also, when you introduce your child to a friend, a teacher, or a new relative, ask your child if he or she wants to shake the person's hand or give them a hug. Don't tell them to. Empower them to know they have a choice from day one.

There are physical signs too. Blood on underwear, illness, soreness, even sexually transmitted diseases that may be misdiagnosed as something else due to the age of the child. You may hear a parent encouraging, "Oh, just hug your uncle Paul. C'mon—he won't bite." Parents should consider that there may be a reason for the child's apprehension. Usually, there is a reason for a child to hesitate to hug a grown woman or man. The child should be free to be a child and not forced to offer affection to a grown-up out of "respect" or to save face for reasons of pride.

Another symptom of sexual abuse to watch for is personality changes. Is your child acting out of character? If your child loves something and gives it up out of the blue, duly consider why that might be. Question the child. Is something wrong? I quit football, basketball, baseball, and soccer so I could focus on karate. It was because Jeff told me to spend more time on it. I loved those other sports, and it was a huge red flag that my parents completely missed. Why would I quit the sports I loved? My coach made me do so for his own interests; that's why. Once the dust settled after the shooting, I went right back into the sports I loved, becoming a four-sport letterman my senior year in high school.

When I talk to parents, I always counsel them on the behavioral changes to watch for:

- Unexplained mood swings
- Changes in eating habits
- Recurring nightmares
- Inappropriate play (sometimes sexual with toys)
- New fears of people
- Secrets they aren't allowed to tell you
- Resuming childlike behaviors (like bed wetting, thumb sucking, etc.)
- Unusual anxiety and clinginess

You know your child best. Don't dismiss weird and unusual behavior. It could be the clue that leads you to helping your child and stopping someone from abusing them.

Consider the following: You attend the monthly family barbecue, and the kids are all outside, playing—all but one.

Your little girl looks up at you and buries her face in your pant leg. She doesn't want to go outside. "What's wrong, sweetie?" She clings to you tighter. You look at her face and see sadness and fear.

Not at all a normal behavior for your child. You kneel down and look her in the eyes. "Why don't you want to go play outside with your cousins?"

"I can never tell anyone . . . ever."

"You can tell me, honey; I am your mommy. Mommy gets to know all of the secrets."

"Are you sure I can tell you?" She looks around, hoping no one can hear her.

"Mommy is sure. Tell me what's wrong, sweet pea."

She tells you that her cousin has been touching her. You are shocked and brokenhearted and quite literally sick. It blows your family apart when you go talk to your brother and sister-in-law about their son.

It is a sad truth that 90 percent of molestation is committed by a family member or someone known to the family.

More than 50 percent of children will wait up to five years to tell someone what is going on. The John Jay Catholic-priest study found that the average time children waited to disclose was twenty years, while 25 percent waited thirty years. Only 13 percent reported in the first year, and many of them were either not believed or not investigated before it was made more widely known that they had been abused. You must know what to look for and how to create an environment of safety.

We must accept the harsh realities that statistics convey, like the following from the Centers for Disease Control and Prevention's website: one in three women and one in four men have experienced sexual violence involving physical contact at some point in their lives.

If you know three girls under eighteen, the chances are high that one of them has been molested. These numbers are staggering. It brings into focus that we truly need to be paying attention. Your best defense is to teach your young children about their bodies, teach them that their own body belongs to them, teach them what is appropriate and inappropriate, and reinforce the proper boundaries.

I attended the Campus Prevention Network's national conference 2018 in New Orleans, and one college reported that 19 percent of their incoming freshmen reported being raped before enrollment, and 40 percent of their students reported being raped after enrollment. Who wants to send their daughter to an institution that is going to double her chances of being raped?

Also, there are a number of studies that state that one in four girls and one in six boys will be molested before they are eighteen. I think boys underreport because of fear of being considered gay and fear of being looked at as a future sex offender. My feeling is that since male offenders who prey on adolescent male victims are the most prolific offenders by far, the number of boys who are molested and never report may be higher than the number of girls who are molested. Boys cannot get pregnant when they are raped; girls can. So there can be more outward evidence with girls. I believe that is what skews the reporting toward girls. Also, we keep our girls away from alone time and overnight alone time with adult males, but we don't do that with our boys. I am living proof that it is easy for a man to get a boy alone. It would be a lot harder to do the same with an eleven-year-old girl.

In some situations, you will be able to prevent it. But when you can't, you can create a safe place for your children to come to and seek help. This can change the duration of abuse. When parents see the warning signs and provide their children with that safe place to recover, they can improve their child's self-image later. You create a life raft that helps them get to shore.

CHAPTER 13:

Survivor

An estimated 33 percent of girls and 20 percent of boys experience sexual abuse before they turn eighteen years old. These statistics are clearly startling. We have avoided thoughtful consideration and open discussions about this awful truth. It's time for us to honestly confront it. I've found that there are many misconceptions and much perpetuated naivete regarding predators. We tend to want to believe the best of other people.

Could your child be at risk of becoming a statistic? The numbers above certainly suggest they are. I am here to do my best to make sure they remain safe—or at least to provide you with as much information as possible to prevent it from ever occurring.

I confess that I didn't speak out against sexual abuse initially because I was twelve years old. Survivors generally don't want to talk about their pain until much later, when they can look at it reflectively and put it in context of their overall life experience. Abuse victims become accustomed to not speaking up about what happened. It takes time to get to the point that you feel safe talking about it to anyone. It's also hard to predict how someone will react to your story; we don't want to make people uncomfortable.

In June of 1997, after graduating from LSU, I moved back to Irving, Texas, where I had attended North Lake College in 1992 and 1993. One night, while searching online for jobs involving sexual-abuse prevention, I found the perfect job.

In May of 1998, I decided to pack up and move to Pennsylvania, partially to escape living under the large and daunting shadow of my father and our family story. Unlike so many other Americans, I had found the exact job I had been looking for. I would be working in Norristown, Pennsylvania, at the Victim Services Center of Montgomery County Inc. just outside of Philadelphia. It was time for me to begin writing this new chapter of my life as a survivor in a new place. I would begin again, far away from the ground zero where I had been almost entirely and singularly known as the victim of a horrible crime. When your dad kills your rapist on national television, everyone knows you on sight. But they don't know who you really are. It can be difficult to be known as anything other than the label people place on you.

In Pennsylvania, I found the freedom of a fresh start without those labels. No one knew who I was or what I had been through. Also, it was agency policy not to disclose any personal abuse if you had been affected directly or indirectly. My story only became known after the massive Catholic Church sex scandal in 2002.

After I watched the disturbing story unfold on the news, I called my friend Art Harris at CNN and said that I wanted to raise awareness for sexual abuse. I told him that it was an important topic to start more conversations about . . . and I wanted to help. I had to discuss my intentions with the executive director of the Victim Services Center—my boss,

Mary Onama. I disclosed my story to her. Then I told her that CNN wanted to do a story.

She thought that was a great idea, so she went to the Victim Services Center board and informed them, "Jody has a friend who wants to use his personal tragedy to bring awareness to sexual abuse. Can we do a story on it?"

They said, "Yes. Absolutely."

Art Harris had worked for the *Washington Post* in 1984 and had written an in-depth article about my situation a few days after the shooting. Over the years he'd stayed in touch with my family in hopes of pitching the story to Hollywood for a made-for-TV movie or feature film. So he knew the story well since he had been there from the beginning.

Art thought it was a great idea to produce an update on the kid who had been kidnapped and sexually abused, whose father had shot the molester on TV, and who had then gone on to do work to prevent sexual abuse. I realized that it wasn't enough just working in Montgomery County, Pennsylvania. I knew there was a world of people out there who needed to hear my story. Possibly more importantly, I also knew that there were children whose parents needed to hear my story so the parents could hopefully protect their children from harm. Or at least rescue them from it.

One thing I've learned on this journey is that you can evolve from being a victim, to a survivor, to an educator. This transformation was essential for me, my mind-set, and my future. If true success is giving back and using your testimony to change lives, then I know that my success will lie in the fact that I've educated parents around the world on what to look for and what not to do. There are very real dangers out there.

Art and his crew flew down and conducted an interview and filmed me doing our Keeping Touches Safe and Healthy program with a second-grade class at Brooke Elementary in Royersford, Pennsylvania—with the parents' permission, of course. During the filming, I was covering the part of the program titled Secret Touching. Secret touching is the inappropriate sexual touch of an adult on a child.

Suddenly, this little boy raised his hand. Normally, I would not have called on him because I wanted to let the students know how serious this information was. But I felt pressure. Pressure because I had the teacher, guidance counselor, producer, the film guy, the sound guy, and Art all watching me. So I made the mistake of calling on him.

He proceeded to smile, put his hand up to his mouth, and uttered, "Sometimes, you can secret touch yourself."

My immediate thought was, "You're telling me, kid. I'm thirty and single." I kept my composure and said, "If you are touching yourself, it is not a secret." I did not want to ruin his teenage years where many young boys spend time "secret touching" themselves.

Next, there was a walk and talk through Valley Forge National Historical Park. Then they filmed me pretending to do work at the office, and we had a sit-down interview in the hallway at the Victim Services Center. Mike Barnett was also interviewed back in Baton Rouge. The segment eventually aired on *Connie Chung Tonight* over the Christmas holidays. I thought it was very well done and well received.

Online, the dangers can be more threatening. Pedophiles are everywhere on the internet, especially in chat rooms. Did you know there are more than five hundred thousand predators online every day? Children ages twelve to fifteen are most susceptible of being manipulated by offenders. FBI statistics show that more than 50 percent of victims of online offenders are within that age group. Children may believe that they are speaking to their peers, but too often that is not the case. It's important that you closely monitor activity and start educating minors as young as possible about what is appropriate online behavior.

However, we sometimes tend to focus so intensely on strangers that we ignore the friends and relatives in plain sight. A child is more likely to be abused by someone they know because the pedophile already has access—that manipulation of trust is already set in stone.

I feel the weight of every victim of sexual abuse because I know how deep the pain goes. I want to do everything I can to protect other children and expose blind spots to parents. At the time of the sexual-abuse scandal involving the Catholic Church around 2002, I needed to be able to reach more people.

That, for me, was the tipping point. I began speaking at fundraisers. That progressed to board members inviting their friends and pillars of the community. I would share my story and show the segment that had aired on *Connie Chung Tonight*. I informed my audiences that I wanted to raise awareness. I told them it was important to help victims resist the tendency to adopt the outlook that their world had ended. I sought to empower individuals who had been fed the lie that life can't go on after their abuse. Too many people stay trapped inside of that idea. Our present culture supports the notion that you can't move on, you cannot evolve, you are changed forever, you are forever a victim. *That is simply not true!*

I know it is not true because I overcame it for myself through hard work, support, and struggle. When I first moved to Pennsylvania, I was making twenty thousand dollars a year. That isn't much money there, but I made it happen. I succeeded because I chose to see a future free of my past. I chose a future not colored by the lens of being a victim but rather by the view of a survivor who would overcome that experience. I would overcome that story that someone else had written for me, and I would now create my own true story.

In December of 2004, I was nominated for the Survivor/Activist of the Year by the Pennsylvania Commission on Crime and Delinquency. It was a great surprise, and my family was there to see me accept the award. My mom, my dad, and a family friend were all sitting in the audience. When they announced my name, I walked up on stage. "I am so honored to receive this award. The reason why someone who has been through what I have been through goes into this line of work isn't for recognition. We don't do this so someone will give us an award. We do it for the money," I said jokingly. There were tons of social workers in the audience, and most of them were hardly earning anything.

Everyone in the room laughed because we are in this for the change we can bring. We don't do this for the money. We pursue this calling in a lasting manner for the lives that can be positively impacted.

Social workers make a tremendous positive contribution to the lives of people touched by abuse. Even when a sexual-assault advocate shares a story without a solution, it helps other victims feel less isolated by providing a connection. These advocates may not always offer solutions or a perspective that life continues, but they do provide a connection to others who have had similar experiences.

At the Campus Prevention Network's 2018 conference in New Orleans, I had the opportunity to hear Tarana Burke speak as the featured keynote speaker. Tarana Burke is an African American civil rights activist from the Bronx, New York, who founded the #MeToo movement to raise awareness of the pervasiveness of sexual abuse and assault in society, and the phrase developed into a broader movement. As she said in her keynote, "This movement is not about taking down powerful celebrities; this movement is about *healing*." She was one of the few sexual-abuse-survivor speakers who did not go into detail about her abuse. She mentioned it. But I appreciated her message of *healing*. She also knows you can be okay.

For me, sharing my story is about sharing hope. It is about sharing the lesson and the truth that you can grow and move on. When I share my story, it is more than connecting with others who have had similar experiences. My sharing is about giving victims proof that abuse is not the end of their lives. They can recover and triumph. They can heal. #MeToo.

People in this field chose this vocation to make a difference. Most knew someone who had been abused, or they were abused themselves. It is about helping people who have survived molestation, rape, or sexual abuse. Despite the stigma, despite the trauma, you can move on and still do incredibly well with your life.

CHAPTER 14:

Grooming

Grooming is behavior aimed at the intended child victims and those who are responsible for their well-being as well as the community that they operate in. Grooming is a constellation of otherwise innocent-appearing behavior that is intended to give a person ongoing access to children for sexual purposes as well as to prevent discovery by others.

These alternative behaviors that sexual offenders illustrate are not always limited to sex. There are more obscure traits of sex offenders that are also disturbing because they resemble traits of truly caring people. Characteristics such as patience, concern for children, and nurturing and investing time in a child. In this fast-paced, rushed world where parents juggle too many responsibilities, the exterior traits of a sexual offender can appear positive, even though their motives are not.

A major misconception is the idea that sex offenders immediately begin molesting their victims. If this were the case, more kids would come forward in the beginning. More parents would notice rapid changes.

Instead, it is a slow, calculated process. It takes time because a pedophile will invest in the victim's family and nurture the relationships to ensure that once the family trusts the predator, any of the victim's symptoms are more difficult to label and notice.

Jim Clemente, a former top FBI profiler, knew the sad truth about "grooming" behavior in child molesters. He wrote the *Clemente Report* on child sexual victimization. It is one of the most comprehensive articles ever published about child sexual abuse.

Clemente states the following four hallmarks of child sex offenders:

1. Long-term persistent patterns of behavior
2. Specific sexual interests
3. Well-developed techniques
4. Fantasy and desire-driven behavior

Jerry Sandusky, a retired football coach and serial rapist, provides us with a textbook example of a predator's grooming techniques. When a pedophile implements the grooming process, he or she seduces the family, the community, and everyone around the child. The child is not the only one subjected to the manipulation. One of the ways that Sandusky kept everyone believing he was just a "nice guy" was that he created a foundation for underprivileged youth. He was a foster parent, a pillar of the community. He had gone to tremendous lengths to groom not just his coworkers, but caseworkers, social services, the community, and, of course, the parents of the children whom he victimized. The school officials all believed Sandusky to be a great guy. When it all came out and the extent of his crimes was revealed, the entire community learned they had been manipulated and deceived as to his true nature.

Clearly, as Sandusky's case illustrates, when a pedophile or sex offender grooms people, he or she is thorough. The family thinks that he or she is just a great person. They say all these great things. The predators may be Boy Scout leaders, they may be coaches, and they can be pillars of the community and appear to be fantastic people. Once you are in that sphere of manipulation and outward appearance, it is difficult to view them objectively. These predators work hard to earn trust. They are masters of emotional manipulation. When I was ten years old, one of the things my karate teacher told my parents was that he loved kids so much because he couldn't have his own children. He told them there was an accident when he was seven years old, and it ruined his chances of having children. It changed my parents' view and created a false sense of security and safety in their minds. They gave Jeff full access to me and my brother without a second thought. This meant warning signs they might have seen went completely unnoticed.

By the time a predator starts taking advantage of a child, they have laid deep and solid foundations of trust and earned affection. The victims are already invested in the relationship and do not want the predator to get in trouble. It's a myth that all children who are molested don't tell because they are threatened. In some extreme cases the abuser does use threats, but more commonly, they use love and affection. When my karate teacher was grooming me, he never threatened to kill me, or my family, or my pets. It was a subtle, methodical approach. He gained my trust, then my affection, and only after those steps were taken would he subtly begin to test my boundaries. He would do small things to test and push those boundaries. For instance, in karate you have to be flexible. He would put us in a split position, and he would adjust me by grabbing my inner thighs. He was testing those boundaries and gauging my reactions. The very first time he tested my boundaries was when he offered to teach us kids how to drive. We were excited! I threw my hand up and wanted to be the first one to get to drive a car. He sat me on his lap in the driver's seat, and that is when he touched me the first time, and my brain threw up a red flag. I told myself, "This is one of those people my mother told me about." As a child, if you haven't been equipped with how to handle that situation, then you don't do anything at all. In that moment, you have no voice.

It's important to note that one of the most effective grooming tools used by offenders to minimize the chances that a child victim will disclose the abuse is to get the child to do something, however small, that the child knows is wrong. With young males, it's typically the three *D*s. Drinking, driving, and dirty pictures. Offenders know that kids want to be treated like adults and look up to them. They want to experience the things that only adults get to do. So offenders often offer opportunities to drink alcohol, drive a car, and look at dirty pictures to children who are underage for those activities. The benefit to the offender is that once a child does something they know is wrong, the likelihood that they will then run home and tell their parents, "I did something wrong; then something bad happened to me" is greatly reduced. This also adds to guilty feelings on the part of the victim. They typically feel that the bad things that the offender did to them were likely caused by the fact that they (the child) did something bad first and that they deserved what happened to them afterward.

It just progressed from there. Jeff was a master of manipulation. In order to get me alone, he would tell the other seven kids in the karate class to take some money, and he would send them to get candy and Icee's across the street. With me, he would say, "Jody, you need to work on extra kicks." That is when he would do it. He would take me to the back room, and just like that, it would be over. Then the kids would come back from the store and find me wiping tears from my eyes. I didn't know what to do, so I wouldn't say anything about it.

When this happens, we expect a ten-year-old to come forward and tell his or her parents that something is going on. Yes, the child was hurt, but this is not like when a child gets a skinned knee and runs into your arms with tears racing down his or her cheeks. The pain of being molested is extremely confusing and isolating. As adults, we cannot assign responsibility for this to a child. Parents need to watch for those signs. Often, they miss those red flags because they are spending too much time with the predator. This is one of the dangers of using the term *predator*. When people think of predators, they think of lions and tigers and bears. They don't think of the nice-guy pillar of the community whom they are willingly handing their kids over to and trusting them with. We have to change that dynamic. I believe the first step is to stop calling them *predators*. Maybe call them wolves in sheep's clothing. We try to train kids when they are old enough to understand that if someone touches their privates, they need to tell a grown-up. We need to be proactively educating parents not to let their kids around people who could touch them. If the coach says, "I can bring them home," you reply, "No, I am going to pick them up." The parents need to be there with them during these activities. Because if you don't take your kids and pick them up, then you run the risk of your child being alone with someone who has different motives than you think.

I know you can't protect and hide kids from everyone. But you also cannot expect that everyone you know is safe just because you know them or perhaps even love them. Children are abused by cousins, siblings, uncles, aunts, and even their own and other parents. A sad fact is that most parents think that it won't happen with a sibling or a close relative. This is exactly the issue. Parents: *Do not* assume that kids will be safe with family or close friends. Your safest avenue is to be present with your children. You surrender the ability to keep them from danger when you abandon your responsibility and hand it off to someone else.

I also acknowledge that it cannot always be that way, but it must be limited. My older brother called me to see if I could take his son to his middle school basketball game. I was available, and I took him. After, we went for Fleur de Lis Pizza (the best pizza in Baton Rouge), and then we went to the LSU vs. Florida basketball game that night. He got a picture with LSU's legendary coach Dale Brown and former LSU great Mahmoud Abdul-Rauf (formerly Chris Jackson while at LSU). We had a wonderful time, but that is the only time it has happened. Remember, if someone wants to spend more time with your kid than you do, that's a *huge* red flag.

CHAPTER 15:

Sexual Abuse and Acting Out

A child's actions can act as a megaphone to indicate there is something wrong. Based on a child's individual personality, abuse can reveal itself in many different ways. Sometimes when a child molests another child, it isn't because that child is already a pedophile. It isn't the same thing as an adult who preys on youth. There is a difference between sexual abuse and acting out.

When I was working at the Victim Services Center, a coworker was on the sexual-abuse hotline when a mother called in and said that she had gotten a call from the school informing her that her daughter had drawn a turtle with an erect penis. When the teacher had asked the little girl what it was, she'd replied, "It's a dick." Now that isn't something you expect to hear from a six-year-old. After the call, I advised my coworker to talk to the mother. She called, and the mom wanted to know if it was possible her daughter had been sexually abused. My coworker told her there was a high probability of it. The mother explained that her nine-year-old son had been previously sexually abused. A few weeks later, I was saddened to learn that the mother had called back and informed us she had found out her nine-year-old son was having sex with his sister. He was acting out sexually with his sister because he had been sexually abused. My heart is broken for that family, but at the same time, it validated my mission of communicating with as many people about sexual abuse as is possible.

Sexually abused children can reach out and introduce that abuse to other children. They act out those things they learned because they know some of it feels good. The misperception that goes with sexual abuse is that since it is abuse, it can't feel good. That is a dangerously misinformed line of thinking. The natural human response to stimuli of a sexual nature, to some extent, is pleasure. We have to make sure that in understanding what a child is going through, we communicate to them that there is nothing at all wrong with them or who they are. Your response is everything to them at that moment. You must communicate with the child that they didn't know any better and that it's not their fault. Their response was physiological, not psychological. The human body reacts naturally to stimulation, and it isn't something for which you, as a survivor of any sexual trauma, should blame yourself. If you had those responses of pleasure at a young age, it wasn't that you enjoyed being taken advantage of.

Teaching children that a reaction is just a natural response reinforces in their minds that their response was normal, but what happened was not. This will reduce the resulting shame in a child's mind as they wonder whether their response was wrong. If they carry less shame, they will also tend to blame themselves less for what happened. This reduction in shame and self-blame will help inhibit sexual problems later. No one should feel responsible for a biological function that is completely natural.

CHAPTER 16:

What Do Predators Look For?

Cracks. Brokenness. Predators look for ways to wedge themselves in by filling a vacuum, touching a weakness, fulfilling a need. They may also look for independence, overachieving, risk-taking, and other positive traits that they can exploit as well. Are you or your children at risk for being prey to a sexual predator? I didn't think we were, nor did my parents.

Child molesters look for specific traits when they are choosing a victim, such as families that are split up or have an absent father. Dating websites are a magnet for predators looking for women who post that they have kids. These single women are at a disadvantage. My father had a drinking problem. Shortly after Jeff started molesting me, my parents split. Mom decided she'd had enough of my dad's drinking, so she made him move out. When faced with negative consequences, an alcoholic will keep drinking. Sometimes the addiction becomes worse than before.

He went back to sneaking drinks, and eventually, she left him again in 1991. Thankfully, they never divorced, but the reason it is important that you know my mother kicked my dad out is because predators and pedophiles look for vulnerable families. My dad wasn't there. In Jeff's mind and possibly in other people's perceptions, he placed himself in that father-figure position. Being acutely aware of how a pedophile's brain works is something that will help you keep your family safe.

Many pedophiles feel as though they love the child. There are also sadistic pedophiles and a spectrum of offenders in between. It becomes an obsession. They feel that the child is who they are meant to be with. In this way, a pedophile's basic "wiring" is wrong. I am not justifying it, but just imagine that you are born with a physical attraction to children. It isn't right that they prey on children, but in their broken minds, it is what they want, and somehow, it isn't wrong to them. If they did think it was wrong, then they would be less likely to commit the act. This is why recognizing the signs that someone is preying on your children and manipulating your family is so important. Because the pedophile doesn't think what they are doing is wrong, they feel no compulsion to explain that they are in love with your child. It is natural to them, and in their miswired and misfired thinking, it is only between them and the child and is none of your business. They view it as no different than when an adult falls in love with another adult. You must be on guard.

You also cannot underestimate the emotional connection that a child molester will create with a child. I felt like I had lost a friend when my father killed the man who'd molested me. I was genuinely upset. He had been like my best friend except that he'd had this one problem that I'd wished he would stop . . . raping me. Think of it from a child's perspective: He took us to movies and AstroWorld. He was a nice guy. Once a day for thirty minutes, I had to put up with this monster, but other than that, he was fun to be around. That can be really confusing to a kid. Your parents don't explain to you that someone is going to come along and be nice, give you gifts, take you fun places, and then molest you.

As parents, our first priority is to protect our children. We warn our children about the dangers of child molesters and "stranger danger." We give them the entire walk through of bad touching and telling us if something happens. Unfortunately, the result of these traditional warnings is that we leave our children perilously unsuspecting of the greater threat of those close to them. We teach our children not to talk to strangers, but strangers are not the greatest threat. It isn't just the dirty old man at the park. It can be those who are closest to us. We need to teach children that it is okay to say no to inappropriate behavior from fathers, aunts and uncles, parents' best friends, and teachers. It is an important message because when we communicate this to kids, they realize that no matter who it is, crossing those boundaries is wrong, and they don't have to keep silent.

Everyone is taught to say no to strangers. People are not typically taught to say no to people they trust: their fathers, mothers, aunts, uncles, or family friends. What is worse is that, as a child, you expect your parents to notice. I had expected my parents to realize what was happening to me much sooner. Just the change in my personality should have tipped them off. To me it was obvious. I couldn't understand why no one could figure this out. I was eleven; I knew there was something wrong with the guy. I knew that a normal twenty-three-to-twenty-five-year-old man shouldn't go around hanging out with kids my age. Jeff would fly into jealous rages if I spent too much time with my father. He would go as far as to accuse me of loving my dad more than him. Through this grooming and manipulation, I gave up activities I loved. I had always been active in sports. Eventually, I withdrew from everything besides Jeff and karate because of the heavy and persistent guilt trips he continued to put on me. This is another perfect example of coercive control.

Sometimes, Jeff abused me while twenty other children played in the next room, either at the karate school or in the joined room at a hotel on our karate trips. No matter how bad things were, I never told anyone. I didn't want to be the one to tell on him. I was afraid of him. I kept thinking my family would figure it out, take me to the hospital, and have me checked out. There they would find I'd been abused, and it would end. I was waiting. But it didn't end. Not until I was kidnapped and then brought home.

CHAPTER 17:

Reactions

In a parent's mind, nothing is worse (other than death) than finding out someone is molesting your child . . . especially someone you trusted. As previously mentioned, your reaction to what happens to your child shapes the behaviors your child will adopt. It is natural to want to react to the emotions that flood your senses: anger, disgust, sadness, and guilt. All of the *whys* and *what-ifs* begin to overwhelm you. If you think this is the worst thing that could ever happen, then that is what you will showcase to your child. Remember, children mirror their parents' reactions. You cannot bring your personal issues to the table when your child goes through this. You are the adult, and this is your child's issue and their table. The role of a parent is to focus on the best way to help the child. Despite the pain and anger, parents must remain calm and help the child respond in his or her own way. A parent's reaction either creates peace and space to recover with less difficulty, or it can create shame and pain, making the recovery from trauma harder.

Sometimes, depending on the age of a child and the circumstances of the event, the victim can have an unclear recollection of what happened or no recollection at all. Most of the time the reaction of the parent is more traumatic to the actual victim. The same thing goes for rape victims. The reactions of the public, the courts, and the people around them can be far more traumatic than the event itself. If someone was drugged or drunk and doesn't remember an event, then they come to base their reaction on the reactions of those around them.

I know someone whose daughter was drugged and raped. She had no recollection of the event. The reaction of outside influences was all she had as a basis to shape her feelings about the incident. The daughter was a teenager, and after the public found out about another teenager drugging and raping her, teens took to social media to bully the victim. When her mother reacted as though it was the worst thing that could ever happen, that is what it turned into. The mother's downward spiral of dialogue began to focus on lost identity, being used, being broken, and being ruined. The girl was left with an overwhelming sense that she could never get over what had happened. Despite the girl having no memory of the attack, the reaction of her mother put her in a position to feel that she could never recover. Over the years I have watched her grow into an adult who struggles now with mental health issues, depression, and anxiety. All shaped by the reaction of a parent. Your child trusts you the most, so earn, preserve, and protect that trust.

When the rape kit came back from the California Police Department in 1984, the police told my mom what had happened. She was shocked and devastated. She cried and fell apart, but not in front of me. She sat me down and calmly said, "Mike Barnett came over today, and the results of the rape kit came back positive."

I pretended to be naive, and I asked her, "What does that mean?"

She said, "That means Jeff fooled with you."

I finally began to tell her everything. Despite the severity of what I shared and the emotions she must have been feeling, she remained calm on the surface. She hugged me and then sent me outside to play with my friends. Her lack of a negative response created a sense of peace in me and an understanding that life still goes on. I went outside to play. She gave me space and encouraged me to work through it on my own time. Now when people ask me the question of how I could possibly recover from being molested, I inform them that I had a bad year and that it didn't ruin my life.

If you are a parent, you have a responsibility to your child's recovery to provide them the tools they need to process the trauma.

What kind of language do you use? What kind of conversations are you having? The language you use around your kids is what shapes their reactions. Consider the impact of telling your child, "If someone ever touches you, I will kill them!" What kind of seed are you planting in your child's mind about you? You are teaching your kid that you might be able to murder someone. You create a fear that tells them if someone touches them, even a family member, that the child would be responsible for someone's death if they told. If someone you loved did something inappropriate and you thought reporting it would get them killed, then you would likely keep that secret forever.

I got a letter once from a woman who wrote, "I told my daughter if somebody ever touches you inappropriately, it's not murder. It's worse than murder. It kills a child's soul." Do you think that little girl would ever open up if she were molested? She doesn't tell anyone because, in her mind, she doesn't want her soul to die and for people to think it died.

My dad said the same thing.

He was too extreme. He would tell anyone who would listen, "If anybody ever touches my kid, I'll kill him." I knew he wasn't kidding. So I didn't tell anyone. When he found out what happened, killing Jeff was exactly what he ended up doing.

Don't be a catalyst for your child not opening up to you.

Your words matter. The way you use them to talk to your children about these types of abuse matters. The words, the conversations, the reactions . . . these things matter. Each of these can have either a positive or negative impact on the victim's perception of what happened, and that can affect the depth and their ability to recover.

CHAPTER 18:

Coping

How do you cope when something bad happens?

Do you know someone who has been raped or molested at some point in their life? There is a high probability that you do. Rape and molestation happens to one in three women and one in five men. (I believe that the real numbers are probably higher.) Chris Anderson of MaleSurvivor told Jim Clemente of a study that showed that 25 percent of all people reported they had been sexually victimized in their lifetime. That's one in four men and women. Think about those numbers. If you know four people, chances are one of them has had some type of sexual trauma.

Creating and using a support system is essential to so many aspects of life. If you don't have a support system, seek or make one. Seek out the compassionate ear of someone close to you. Your family can prove to be a great resource for understanding and managing feelings of guilt and shame. Don't rely solely on yourself to recover. If you have suffered through molestation or rape, you need to realize that recovery doesn't happen overnight. The process is much like the grieving process. You have to realize that in the beginning, emotional swells and crashes could be minute by minute and then hour by hour and day by day. Be patient with yourself. There will be times when your emotions will overwhelm you. Just like coping with the death of a loved one, you will have bad days and good days. Grief can come like waves in the ocean. When the tide goes out, you may feel amazing and have days where you feel as though you have it all together. And when the waves come rushing back in, you may feel overwhelmed. That is normal. It all takes time, and over time it will get easier. There are so many ways that we can cope with a traumatic event. There could be a time after the incident when you are trying to suppress what has happened. When the abuse stops and you try to ignore what happened, the feelings it has caused you can and most likely will come back.

Triggers

A trigger is something that sets off a memory or flashback.

Going through puberty in high school, when you become sexually active, when you become more intimate with someone, or even once you have children of your own, triggers can create problems for you to deal with later.

There are several types of trauma in life and many different ways we can respond.

Several years ago, my godson, Calob, was in a horrific accident that caused him to lose his leg. At the time of the accident, Calob was set to enter his junior year of high school. He was a star football player who'd had a key interception that had helped his team win the state championship just months before.

He endured multiple surgeries and literally hundreds of hours of physical therapy and rehab. Through hard work, determination, and heart, Calob was able to return to the field once again and play in the state championship game his senior year.

Years later, when Calob was attending college, I asked him a question: "Would you rather go through what I went through for a year or lose your leg?"

He shook his head, "Man, I can't answer that," he said.

"Well, try," I said. "What do you think?"

"I don't think I can."

I told him that I knew I could. "I would rather go through what I did for a year at age eleven and have both my legs for the rest of my life."

Let me explain for those of you wondering why I would pose such a terrible question. I am neither minimizing the abuse I suffered nor trivializing my godson's tragedy. Nor is it my intention to compare misfortunes. I am conveying that abuse is not a death sentence, and a child's life isn't over because of it.

Similarly, Calob's life wasn't over because he lost his leg. He had to learn to cope with the loss. He had to grieve and learn to adapt to a much different life than the one he had expected.

The loss of a limb didn't leave him permanently broken. The same can be said of sexual abuse. We all navigate different trails that we didn't choose and cannot control. But we all can choose how we respond to them.

When you are struggling to manage abuse, avoid all forms of self-destructive behavior such as drugs and alcohol, as those will complicate your recovery. Substance abuse will only create more problems.

Substance abuse is a process of self-numbing, which, when used as a coping mechanism, will lead to future problems that will prolong and impair your recovery time. The objective is *overcoming* trauma versus *avoiding* trauma. If you layer over the sexual abuse with substance abuse for twenty years and then finally enter a twelve-step program to recover from the addiction, you will then still have to face the sexual-abuse aspect and learn to recover from it without substances. If you turn to alcohol or drugs, you have created a new problem to deal with, and it will certainly impede the healing process. You can recover! There are so many things in this life that can bring us down, but if you push through and seek the proper help, you can overcome anything with time.

With all that had happened to me in my youth, I had a few choices to make when I went off to college. Some people drink in college—a lot. In college, there were people who knew about what had happened to me. It had been in the news for years, and I didn't keep what had happened a secret. I made the conscious decision not to drink during college. It wasn't because I didn't want to, but rather it was because I didn't want people to mistake my drinking for lack of coping skills. I wanted to set an example for others. I didn't want them to attribute my drunkenness to not being able to handle what had happened in my youth. During my college years, I had appearances on many television shows, including *Geraldo*, *Now It Can Be Told*, *Maury*, *The Oprah Winfrey Show*, *Leeza*, *Real TV*, and *The Montel Williams Show*, as well as the local news. My story was not a secret, and I was in the spotlight. I did not want to validate drinking as a recommended tactic to recover from sexual abuse.

If we had a client at the Victim Services Center who was an active drug user or had an addiction problem, we would tell them that they would have to get clean if they wanted to get help. If they were covering up the problem, then the counseling wouldn't work. If they came in sober, then it was possible to treat them and work on the problems. We found people halted using negative coping mechanisms when they were ready to completely help themselves.

Recovery is something that is earned with hard work. It doesn't happen overnight. You can't just cover up the pain and hide it. Seek that support system: counselors, treatment centers, support groups, and even friends and family. That support system can be there to listen, be in the same space, or even talk you through the process. Recovery can and will happen. You just need to find and use the tools to move forward toward that recovery.

The empowerment philosophy: When someone is helping another person cope with trauma, they can provide the person options on what is the best way to recover. The person in need of recovery must be willing to choose the best option to help themselves mend.

CHAPTER 19:

Myths of Molestation and Rape

There are times in life when something terrible happens, and despite all your explanations, no one will believe you. It is as though you need photographic proof to convince people. Have you had it go so far as them accusing you of being at fault for something that was out of your control?

This is a frequent problem among rape victims. One example is the Steubenville rape situation. In 2012, a young high school girl had become incapacitated by alcohol. Several boys from her school not only raped her but made videos, sent picture messages, posted about it on social media, and shared the videos with their other male friends. Despite the long trail of evidence showing the severity of the situation, not all the boys who participated in this were charged. The parents of the boys who were charged were upset that their young boys would have to suffer the shame of juvenile prison and serve time for what they had done. The public blamed the girl because they felt she had asked for it. They felt she had put herself in that situation. Do you have children who are high schoolers? Can you imagine the public blaming a child for putting herself in a situation to suffer multiple rapes and degrading pictures that were shared everywhere?

There are many situations where a woman has been held accountable rather than the rapist being held accountable. Why does the public turn on the victim? The answer is that it is situational. The below responses indicating that victims are being held accountable stem from the myths that some people believe about rape and molestation. #RapeCulture

Myths of Rape

"It was an accident."

"She didn't say no."

> You *accidentally* lose your keys—you don't *accidentally* rape someone. I am more in favor of the saying "Yes means yes" instead of "No means no." My reason for this is because I should not assume that I can have sex with every woman I see. It is up to a woman to give me consent by saying yes, instead of me forcing sex on any woman I like unless and until she says no.

"Well, look what she was wearing."

> This is stating that someone's clothing choice makes them deserve to be sexually assaulted. I have often said during my programs with the Victim Services Center, "Just because she is dressed to get some doesn't mean she wants it from you!" I also often wonder what percentage of rapes occur at nudist colonies . . . to this day, I have not found those statistics. The truth is that people can dress provocatively and not want to have sex with anyone. They should be allowed

to dress however they want, and that doesn't mean they are looking for sex.

"Look how much she drank."

Drinking isn't an excuse to take advantage of someone, and it isn't an invitation for someone to rape you. If you find yourself in a situation where you know someone has had too much and might be in danger, tell the bartender, offer to take them home, or even call the authorities. Also, if you are at a party and you see someone, whether it be a friend or a stranger, who is incapable of making a decision to consent to a sexual act because alcohol has impaired his or her judgment, be the person to take a stand and help them. Don't be a bystander. It's better to be a "cockblocker" at the party rather than a witness in court for a rape case later!

"I can't stop once I get going."

I've had the opportunity to speak at many high schools and colleges; I asked the students if they thought it was unfair to ask someone to stop in the middle of sex. It was split with girls saying, "Yes, it is fair to say to stop," and the boys responding, "No."

When we asked the boys why it wasn't fair, the general response was, "Once you get going, you can't stop."

My response to this is, "If her dad walked in on you fooling around, I know you could stop." That means that no matter what, you *can* stop. You don't have to force someone to finish something because you think you "need it."

The question to think about is why someone would say stop. Why might this happen? Maybe they were the prior victim of some type of sexual abuse and something triggered a memory? Maybe they got scared of pregnancy? Maybe the intercourse is painful? Maybe they have to take a shit? Whatever reason someone asks you to stop, you must respect their wishes. Not every reason they may have is to leave some guy mad and with blue balls. There could be other, more important reasons.

"No means no."

This campaign is stupid. I don't have the right to have sex with all the girls at Hooters or Twin Peaks and wait for them to say no. No man, woman, or child should have to say no in order for someone not to force themselves on them. If you are incapacitated, mentally ill, or scared of what might happen if you do say no, not being able to say no shouldn't be what places you in harm's way.

"Rape is falsely reported all the time."

If you compare how many rape cases take place versus how many are falsely reported, the incidences are very low. It is no higher for falsely reported rape than any other falsely reported felonies. In fact, rape is one of the most underreported crimes. In nearly 80 percent of cases, the victim knows the person who sexually assaulted them. The US Department of Justice states that at least 63 percent of rape isn't reported to the police. A Washington State study reported that only 20 percent of women who sought post-rape treatment actually reported to the police. So 80 percent went unreported.

"Rape doesn't happen that often."

The statistics don't lie. The National Sexual Violence Resource Center reports that one in three women and one in five men will be victims of sexual violence at some point in their lives. Look at the contact list of friends you have on your cell phone. Do you know three women? Further, one in three girls and one in six boys will be sexually abused *before* they turn eighteen years old.

"Every person who is raped should be crying hysterically if they were really raped."

Not true—everyone responds to trauma differently. Some will cry while some people will be quiet. The myth is that they are going to appear beat up and be crying. What if it was a spouse or a friend who raped them? The victim could be in a state of shock, which causes them to shut down instead of exploding into hysterics. People often like to point out that someone must have lied about being raped if they do fun things after the fact. Just because someone seeks to continue with their life doesn't make them liars.

"Men are not the victims of sexual assault."

Most men who are sexually assaulted are assaulted by other men. In 2014, of the more than seven hundred reported cases of teacher-on-student sexual victimization in the US, 33 percent of the offenders were female. Women are responsible for a significant portion of rapes in this country. Mainly against boys, but against girls too.

"Being sexually assaulted by someone of the same gender will make you become homosexual."

That simply isn't true. That is a common question that I get asked because of what happened to me. It didn't make me gay, nor is that what will happen to someone else. Reactions to what happened will vary, but it isn't an automatic change in a person's sexual orientation. Studies have shown that a person is born homosexual.

People would always speculate that I might be gay from what happend with Jeff. But I would tell people, "I know for a fact I am not gay. I sucked a dick before and didn't like it." That would make them feel uncomfortable enough that the conversation would never come up again.

As Seinfeld said, "We're not gay—not that there's anything wrong with that. I mean, it's fine if that's who you are. I have many friends who are gay."

"People with disabilities are unlikely to be sexually assaulted."

Not true. They are at higher risk because they can't defend themselves. Some of them can't speak up or even say no. Another reason the "No means no" campaign is illogical. If someone is unable to communicate or doesn't have the ability to care for themselves, this doesn't mean they deserve for someone to take advantage of their vulnerability. There is an excellent documentary on HBO called *Mea Maxima Culpa: Silence in the House of God*. The film details the first-known protests against clerical sexual abuse in the United States, initiated by four deaf men. It also pointed out how one pedophile priest would only molest deaf children whose parents did not know sign language—basically making it impossible for them to tell their parents. I recommend going to watch it right now. You can finish this book later.

The best example I can think of is the case of Nathan Sutherland, a licensed nurse at Hacienda HealthCare in Phoenix, Arizona. He was arrested in 2019 after a woman who was incapacitated and partially in his care gave birth. DNA matched him to the baby, and he was charged with sexual assault and abuse of a vulnerable adult. Incapacitated people cannot give consent.

"Prostitutes can't be raped."

Yes, they can. The problem lies in the fact that they're already engaging in something illegal. It becomes hard for the police and law enforcement to do anything to help. Prostitutes lack the ability to protect themselves because of the illegal activity they are already involved in. This is another reason why I support "Yes means yes." A prostitute can consent to which sexual acts she chooses to participate in. But if she is not paid for the agreed-upon act, what is the crime?

Speaking of prostitutes, escorts, prostitution, and human trafficking, in November of 2016, my brother and I drove to Corpus Christi,

> Texas, to attend a friend's wedding. On the way he made me listen to an interview by Jason Ellis on his *Ellismania* podcast. He interviewed a human-trafficking survivor named Rebecca Bender. She was a victim of human trafficking and was forced to be an escort in Las Vegas. It is a must listen and can be found by a simple Google search. If you want to have your mind changed about prostitution and how they should be charged, or if you think it should be legalized, listen to it, and you will forever see the world's oldest profession in a different light. I am all about consent. The problem is that most if not all prostitutes are not consenting of their own free will. They have some pimp or handler controlling them. Go listen.

We have all heard the above phrases. We cannot continue to support rapists by supporting this lexicon of lies. An observation from my years of working with people in crisis services is that people who suffer through multiple traumas will do whatever it takes to survive. The problem with doing whatever it takes is that the way they choose may not always be a healthy behavior. Drugs, alcohol, sexual addiction, and violence are a few things people engage in to cope with continued traumatic events. With a culture that supports rapists and places the blame on victims, we have to take a different approach and claim responsibility for ensuring that we are not afraid to talk about rape and about molestation. When that happens, there can be healing.

CHAPTER 20:

Sex Education and Sexting

As parents, aunts, uncles, and even close family friends, when we think of the teenagers in our lives, we don't want to think of them having sex. The average age in the United States for losing your virginity is seventeen. That means some teens are having sex sooner, and some teens are waiting until they are older.

Laws vary from state to state on what constitutes rape. This creates great confusion when reporting rape. It is more than understandable that we, as parents, don't want our children having sex until they are eighteen—or never, even. Realistically, we need to be prepared for the possibility that they will have sex. We need to educate them on the subject so they are learning about it from a credible source and not their friends or a sex offender.

Sex education is important for preventing rape, sexually transmitted diseases, and teen pregnancy. We equip them with the knowledge they need to make the right decisions when we educate them honestly about sex and what to expect. When we outsource this critical education to their peers, we are letting the world dictate how they should manage the challenges of puberty and hormones. They will lack the information they need to get through these turbulent times. I believe human-sexuality education needs to be taught in all schools, public and private. And it also needs to be reinforced in the home as well. An excellent resource is *There's No Place Like Home . . . for Sex Education*. Google it.

Another societal factor is technology. Over the last decade, the advent of smart mobile phones has placed every imaginable resource within a few clicks of practically the entire globe's teenagers and children. If their parents and guardians don't educate them with the information and knowledge that they need about sex, they have plenty of opportunities to learn it wherever and however they want.

Technology is being used now for teenagers to share pictures of what is going on in their lives. It sounds positive, but the unfortunate consequence is an unexpected one, and that is sexting. Sexting is the sharing of compromising photos and messages between people, and it has become a popular thing among teens. What is happening now is those images are ending up on more devices than the sender thought they would. If a girl's boyfriend asks her for a naked picture and she sends it, he can easily share that with anyone, including social media and porn sites, which can lead to it going viral, meaning widespread distribution. The wrong person will use this technology as a weapon and brag to their peer group about being able to get the image. Closely following a new behavior are laws, and sure enough there are now great advances in revenge-porn laws, cyberstalking, and cyberbullying. When anyone under the age of eighteen takes, copies, or sends sexualized or naked pictures of themselves or other minors with their phone and via the internet or social media, they are violating federal child-pornography statutes and could be subject to prosecution and imprisonment for twenty years or more for the production and distribution of child pornography.

There have been many large court cases of boys using Dropbox, a common cloud-storage site, to share pornographic pictures or photos of their girlfriends naked. Child-pornography charges have been filed in these cases where kids are sharing these photos all over the web. There were over seventy-five images in the Mecklenburg case. When some of the girls realized what had happened, they went to the principal to have the images and the Dropbox account shut down. The problem was that it had already been up for months of viewing before it was eventually taken down. Months of images that could be potentially damaging not just as a teenager, but as an adult.

Sexting has more consequences than just embarrassment or humiliation. It can lead to shame and guilt for the people who have chosen to participate. If it goes public, it can cause problems with reputation and even create problems with college pursuits and potential future career opportunities. There have been widespread accounts of college admissions and athletic and academic scholarships all being rescinded after such images were discovered. Despite legal proceedings to remove such images, the extent of their damage may not be known till one of the victims is trying to get a job and their potential employer does an internet search. In some cases it can lead to court battles.

Another example of this happened in Canada. The Bridgewater case had five boys go up on criminal charges for using Dropbox to share pornographic images of twenty underage girls at their school.

This really hit home with me in September of 2015 when a graduate of North Penn High School (Montgomery County, Pennsylvania) was arrested for sharing a link of sexually explicit pictures of his female classmates and putting them in a Dropbox account folder called "I Prolly had UR Pics." The student eventually plead guilty and was sentenced to probation and community service.

As the *New York Times* explained, "Teenagers who sext are in a precarious legal position. Though in most states, teenagers who are close in age can legally have consensual sex, if they create and share sexually explicit images of themselves, they are technically producing, distributing or possessing child pornography. The laws passed decades ago that cover this situation were meant to apply to adults who exploited children and require those convicted under them to register as sex offenders."

The *New York Times* goes on to report, "In the past, partners wrote love letters, sent suggestive Polaroids and had phone sex. Today, for better or worse, this kind of interpersonal sexual communication also occurs in a digital format." Unfortunately, unlike before, now these digital images can be copied and transmitted millions of times, and they can live in cyberspace for eternity.

These are just a few examples of how parents missed the opportunity to teach kids what can happen if they choose to share such things. You have the responsibility and opportunity to create meaningful and real dialogue about these subjects. You have the chance to impact how your child reacts when someone asks them for a nude photo. Children and teenagers need to know that there are consequences for the choices they make. Social media can be a great tool for us to create meaningful connections and share information with friends and family. But it is also being used as a tool to exploit children and teenagers. If you don't tell them what could happen in advance, you may find yourself dealing with the damage after the fact.

As a parent, you have the most important role of educator. Equip your children with the tools they need to be aware of the dangers and pitfalls they will face under pubescent peer pressure. That one conversation at the right time could be what prevents them from suffering a massive humiliation. It is also important to remember to tell your children to never take nude photos and think they will get away with it by deleting the photos, because they're never truly deleted. Data is forever—your phone is frequently backed up to servers in the network; email is also backed up by Google, Yahoo, etc. All social media posts, even on messaging platforms such as Kik and Snapchat, are all saved by the companies that manage that software. Investigators can always get into a phone, a network, or a company and retrieve any of its deleted or backed-up files. Modern technology is available to document every mistake children make, so prepare your children to avoid being caught with something that could forever affect their future.

CHAPTER 21:

Bystander Intervention

The world of higher education has been a place that hides rape statistics and does little in the way of helping create a safe place for incoming students every year. The administration at colleges and universities spend their time with their heads in the sand and covering up crime statistics so they don't suffer admissions declines and lose federal and state funding and scholarship programs. Envision that each student will be spending tens of thousands and frequently up to and over six digits during his or her college experience. There could be a massive impact on the school and the community if admissions go down for whatever reason, and certainly crime would be a compelling factor to steer your child elsewhere.

Each year a new group of young male and female adults who may have had everything given to them and may have been taken care of their whole lives are being sent off on their own. Going from living at home with little to no responsibility, these young adults find themselves sitting in a wonderful newfound freedom. They are ill prepared and have not been given the awareness for potential distress and violence that is a possibility on any college campus.

Thankfully, many college and university institutions have mandated a preorientation video class that reviews what potentially dangerous situations look like and how "not" to rape someone. The quality of the presentation is of high importance. But truthfully, I find that these videos and subsequent quizzes are laughable. There is no standardized way to help educate these college students about the problems and dangers of coming into these social institutions. I highly recommend watching the documentary *The Hunting Ground*, which highlights sexual assault on college campuses.

We need to make sure that women entering these situations know that the obvious positives of newfound freedom are socializing with friends, responsible drinking, and the overall college culture. However, there are also many negatives, including that not everyone around them has their best interests at heart. This also applies to young, naive men.

As educators, we need to be making sure that we are doing more to create a safe place for education, not just an institution that ignores rape and sexual abuse and benefits from zero accountability. The National Sexual Violence Resource Center reports that more than 90 percent of sexual assault on college campuses goes unreported.

The office of Missouri senator Claire McCaskill administered a survey of over three hundred four-year colleges and universities. The results showed that over 40 percent of the schools had not conducted a sexual-assault investigation at all in the previous five years. While it would be great to think that since no assault investigations had been filed, no assaults had happened, that would be a naive and ignorant conclusion. The more likely answer is that these instances of potential assault were overlooked, covered up, or ignored. With the potential negative effects that happen to victims when they do report the crime, fewer are coming forward every year—less than 5 percent.

Again, the responsibility always falls back on parents to educate their kids on these threats even and especially as they move into the college age and the associated culture.

Bystander Intervention

The majority of men have the capacity to realize when someone is in danger of being too intoxicated. It is critical that we teach bystanders to see these things and not ignore them. Throughout my career as a sexual-abuse educator and advocate, I have done my best to educate people to know what bystander intervention means and how to put it into practice. I tell the bar owners I have met through my travels, "If you see a girl who is drunk, and some guy says he is going to take her home, get a picture of his driver's license. If something happens, you have documentation." Taking precautions is not a sign of paranoia. Nor is it being suspicious. It is acknowledging the risk and preparing in advance for it. You are trying to reduce the risk of problems and potentially harmful outcomes. That driver's license picture just might be the proof necessary to prevent and solve a problem.

You also need to be aware of your surroundings. No matter what the case. I was traveling one year out on this deserted road in the pitch black, and I went to switch to my satellite radio and swerved, and a police officer flashed his lights at me. So I slowed down, put on my flashers, and drove a mile up to a well-lit gas station. I wasn't going to pull over in the middle of a deserted area when I didn't know who was flashing their lights at me. When the officer questioned why I didn't immediately pull over, I explained, "Officer, I work as a sexual-abuse educator and advocate. I educate my clients always to be aware of their surroundings and to go to a safe, well-lit place. It wouldn't be right if I didn't follow my own advice."

Be aware of your surroundings. I have a friend, Javier Pallais, who used to be a general manager at the local Hooters here in Baton Rouge on Siegen Lane. I was telling him how it bothered me when the girls left work with cash on them, how they would not be paying attention to their surroundings as they walked to their cars. They would walk to their cars while checking their Instagram or Facebook messages. So he decided he would address the situation by following them and grabbing them and scaring the shit out of them to teach them a lesson. This one waitress said, "You will never get me."

Well, one night after she got off of work, he snuck into her car and ducked behind the back seat. Not paying attention, she got into her car, and he popped up and scared her. He was doing it for their own good. It is very important to pay attention to your surroundings.

Stay with the masses. This is important because predators are looking for easy targets.

Use the buddy system. If you are at the club and you want to hook up with someone you like, then let your friends know. If you just want the free drinks and you don't want to hook up, then tell your friends that too. Someone who is looking to assault someone sexually is looking for an easy target. Since 80–90 percent of sexual-assault problems involve alcohol, be aware of what you are consuming. People say that you should be careful of someone putting something such as drugs in your drink. But we should also be mindful of the fact that drinking twelve drinks at the bar isn't recommended. But it is not a crime, and it is not an invitation for rape. It's an invitation for a hangover. No one has the right to assault you, but remember that you can make yourself a less likely target.

An example of bystander intervention happened when a friend of mine, Dave (who once sang backup on a Red Hot Chili Peppers album), and I were in Irving, Texas, at a bar near the Cowboys practice area. This drunk woman with a broken arm started to come on to me. (Come to find out later, she was taking pain meds for her arm but was still drinking.)

We were keeping an eye on her, and we noticed these sketchy guys circling like buzzards. She was laughing and tossing back drinks, no doubt to numb her arm. But it looked like one of those times where if someone didn't intervene, then tomorrow she would be wondering what had happened to her. We knew that if we were going to be sure she was safe, we would need to take her home. She was reaching the level of blackout drunk to the point where we had to dig out her driver's license because she was so drunk she couldn't even tell us where she lived. We got her home, waited till she fell asleep, which was not long, and we left.

The next day we were at work at North Lake College, and we were telling our boss the story, and he said, "Well, did you make sure she is okay?" We hadn't. Dave decided he would go over to her apartment at three in the afternoon to make sure she was okay.

She was so messed up she didn't recognize the guy who had brought her home safely. She had a serious look of concern on her face as she couldn't recollect how she had gotten home or what had happened when she had gotten there. She looked at Dave and said, "Did we have sex?" It is a terrible combination to mix drugs and alcohol. That much alcohol plus her pain medication gave her no recollection of how she had gotten home or what had happened. If we hadn't stepped up and made sure she got home safely, there is no telling what would have happened to her.

This goes to show how so much can happen that we won't be able to recall how to defend ourselves. Imagine if one of the jerks who had been checking her out while she was in a drunken state had taken her home. She could have woken up and had no idea what had happened. Puzzling out a bender is not something anyone should have to do.

Another example of stepping up happened when I went to a party once in Pennsylvania. I was invited to a party that turned out to be just one girl and a bunch of guys. There was a lot of drinking, and a couple hours later, the girl was completely smashed. I knew this was bad news, so I took her and put her in her room and shut the door. The other guys at the party wanted to get in there and mess with her while she was unconscious. I flat out said no. There was no way that a young girl, drunk or not, would be subject to any kind of assault with me there. I ended up staying in the room with the door locked for the night because they wouldn't leave. I was concerned they would do something to her in the state she was in.

When we got up in the morning, the guys had completely ransacked her apartment. It was trashed. They had thrown food everywhere and destroyed her stuff. This was the kind of thing you would expect out of a burglary, not a friendly get together. That behavior told me that had I not intervened, something would have happened to her, and I would have held myself accountable had I seen her on the news. Sometimes, you must step in.

Another time was in 2016 in New Orleans at a retreat for the board members of the Louisiana Foundation Against Sexual Assault. We saw a young lady who was super drunk. I said, "Should we make sure she is okay?" As board members, we certainly couldn't just sit by and watch as someone got wasted without making sure they were safe. We were active participants in what was going on. We checked with her friend to make sure it was all good and that she was safe.

As a bystander intervening, we aren't here to stop people who want to get together from doing it or having fun. We just want to make sure they want to. And it turned out fine. Not every instance is you protecting someone from assault; sometimes it is just making sure someone is safe.

Bystanders intervening used to be called cockblocking. Cockblocking is what happens when someone doesn't get to have sex due to someone interrupting or intervening. If you are intervening with someone who is too drunk and is incapable of giving consent, then it isn't cockblocking; it's preventing sexual assault. If my "cockblocking" prevents someone from being sexually assaulted, raped, or abused, I'll be more than happy to cockblock!

With the invention of such websites as Tinder and Match.com, some bars and clubs have implemented codes you can share with the bartender if you need help. You can order an angel shot and ask for it in the following ways:

- Neat: The bartender will walk you to your car.
- With ice: The bartender will call an Uber or Lyft for you.
- With lime: The bartender will call the police.

There are of course many variations of this, but it all comes down to understanding that you can ask for help. These codes can easily be displayed in the ladies' room, so each bar can have their own codes.

None of the club or bar staff wants to hear that someone was hurt, raped, or assaulted in their establishment. Never be afraid to reach out and ask for help. If someone doesn't turn out to be who they said they were, tell the bartender or the waitress. You are not obligated to stay. Remember, you always have a choice.

CHAPTER 22:

Risk Reduction

How can you prevent your child from becoming a victim? Vigilance is the answer. I have been working in the field of violence prevention since 1995. You can't prevent it. Although you might be able to prevent a particular incident, you can't prevent violence altogether. When you have an alarm on your house, it isn't prevention. It is a risk reduction.

Risk Reduction Techniques

- Buddy system
- Not out after dark alone
- No headphones
- Know your surroundings

Why would you need to do these things?

Fab got out of her car. It was dusk, and she was running late for her evening run. She laced up her running shoes, put in her headphones, and started down the path. It was a well-lit park with forested areas throughout. She just wanted to get in a quick mile before she went out with her girlfriends for the night.

We think about the above scenario, and we can immediately see what is wrong. It's dark, she is alone, and she is unaware of the sounds around her. But how often do we consider that invincible thought, "It will never happen to me"?

There are people in this world who don't care whom they hurt, whether that is through molestation, sexual assault, abuse—you name it. And most of the time you can't prevent something bad from happening because you can't control other people. You can do your part to reduce your risk of being targeted as a victim. When predators are looking for victims, they are looking for an easy target. They aren't looking for a group or for someone who will be aware. They rarely seek out victims during the day unless the victims are by themselves and unaware of their surroundings.

When you go in a pair and don't wear your headphones, you are a group now, and you are aware of your surroundings so no one can sneak up beside you. You can be out at a time of day that isn't conducive to attacks. You can reduce the risk of being assaulted.

Who are easy targets?

College students are huge targets for sexual assault. Young freshman girls or boys who drink at parties can easily drink too much. This impairs their ability to defend themselves. They are also statistically less likely to report it. The US Department of Justice stated that from 1995 to 2013, 80 percent of women who had been sexually assaulted on college campuses didn't come forward and report it. Why? Most people don't want anyone to know it happened to them. And they sometimes blame themselves, saying things like "I brought this on myself" or "I drank too much" or "I dressed wrong" or "I didn't know how to say no."

Some have no idea what is actually considered rape. Victims will internalize what happened and feel ashamed. If it happened with someone they know, then the misconception that rape only happens with strangers and includes abuse or violence convinces them it was not rape. It is rare and difficult for someone to realize that what happened to them was a crime when they knew and trusted the person who assaulted them.

Another reason it goes unreported is that the victim just doesn't think the police will believe them. The US State Department showed that 21 percent of physically forced victims and 12 percent of incapacitated victims did not come forward because they didn't think the police would consider it a serious crime. Also, 13 percent of forced victims and 24 percent of incapacitated victims feared the police would mistreat them as if they'd deserved it. With only 18 percent of reported cases of rape ending in a conviction, victims don't see positive results in coming forward with sexual assault.

With that being said, when do we consider it rape? Is it rape if you are too drunk to say no? People generally aren't sympathetic to the person who goes and drinks too much and then gets raped. If someone is blackout drunk, you have to weigh your cognitive dissonance. Is it rape when someone can't say no? It is a personal choice to decide you are going to go after the drunk girl or guy. If you decide the intoxicated person is your best chance at a "good time," it is probably sexual assault. There is no law that says you should not go out and get blackout drunk, but there is a law against you fucking someone who is blackout drunk!

CHAPTER 23:

Moving Forward

We as humans have an amazing capacity for resilience. One of the reasons that I have become an advocate about sexual abuse is that I want to see the conversation about it change. Without fail, every time I speak and share my story, someone comes up to me and tells me their story.

"I was molested as a kid, and it is what caused me to grow up and be a counselor and an advocate."

"Thank you for speaking about it this way; it is rare for people to come forward and say that this is something that you can move on from."

You have to keep in mind that you never know who has been through rape or molestation. The way you talk about it to friends and family matters. You've got to be careful not to justify sexual abuse by saying it's because someone else was abused growing up or because they're drinking or drunk or any other justification. Victims live with the secret shame of sexual abuse for a lifetime until they're ready to talk about it or until it's exposed. We saw that with the whole #MeToo movement in 2017 and 2018.

Often, I hear people justifying the actions of a rapist (victim blaming) because people need an answer as to why someone sexually abuses someone else. Blaming the victim can weigh heavy on a survivor who may have been able to share their story of abuse with you. Now they feel as though their story must somehow be their fault.

If someone does decide to share their story with you, remain calm. Never ask a "why" question. "Why" questions are indicative of blame. Believe the person, and be supportive by providing them, again, with options. Let them decide what is best for them.

That is what my mother did with me. I had some karate articles that had been on my wall for years, and after the shooting, my dad wanted me to pull all of those things down. My mom was supportive, and she said that I could take them down when I was ready. Thank God for Mike Barnett, his training, and that he told my mom to leave me be and let me go back to how life was before.

With rape and molestation, someone has forced a person to do something . . . as a result of this, you don't want to force a rape victim to do anything. That could put them into a state of rebellion. You become just another person forcing them to do something against their will.

As a child, you may have had something traumatic happen. There is the thought that kids block out bad things. That isn't always the case. At a young age, children may not have the capacity to understand what is happening. If parents respond calmly, a child may move past this event, and it may not come up till far later. Not because they blocked it out, but because that's when the person is ready for it to come out. Children have shorter memories than adults. It may not be something that they think of once it is over until something triggers it later on down the line.

In so many different areas of our lives, we need permission to do something. It seems true for recovering from trauma as well. There isn't always someone who comes out and says, "It's going to be okay" after someone has been through a traumatic event. Since no one has said it, the victim may not feel comfortable with saying it to themselves. We have to break through the silence and the pattern of sensationalizing the trauma of sexual abuse while glossing over the recovery portion as unimportant or impossible.

TV shows sensationalize molestation and the trauma versus the recovery. The focus is on dramatizing the incident because of the shock value it delivers to the audience. But rarely does the story shift the focus to the hope found in the aftermath. However, CBS did a trilogy of episodes of *Criminal Minds* that highlighted the journey of recovery for one of its characters, Derrick Morgan, played by Shemar Moore. In the episodes "Profiler, Profiled," "Foundation," and "Restoration," this series showed the difficult but successful process of Morgan facing his victimization and going on to survive, thrive, and become an outspoken advocate for survivors. Every story has an opportunity of hope. The news channels retraumatize victims through the language used in media. They refer to the victim as an "accuser," "alleged victim," or "complaining witness." All three descriptions influence the viewers' perspectives of the person making the statement. It changes how we see the person who endured trauma and now is enduring public defamation of character for coming forward.

Understanding the dynamics of what happened and how to overcome it is paramount for creating people who can suffer traumatic events and recover. Sexually abused kids will turn into traumatized adults without the proper help.

You must realize that the claim that "you can never psychologically recover from rape or molestation" is only true if you let it be. It is a social fiction that is keeping sexual-abuse victims from recovery. It may be something that you must take moment by moment until you create coping skills that help you overcome it. It doesn't happen overnight. It is just like the grieving process. With the proper support, you can heal. The support and comfort come from family, friends, and counselors. Support may come from a pastor at church or a close friend who went through the same thing. It is all about what helps you.

What is it you've been through in your own life?

Pain is pain. Maybe you've been through a divorce or rejection, and it shattered your world. You cannot let one moment define you. You have to rise up and change and be willing to heal and then put it in the right perspective.

One of the reasons I wanted to write this book after all these years is to be proactive about helping parents know what to say and what not to say to their kids about strangers and about loved ones. Often, I'll hear a parent say, "If that happened to my kid, I would kill someone." But if your child doesn't want you to kill someone or go to prison for murder, why would they tell you? A child doesn't want to be responsible for someone being killed. As a result, kids come to their own conclusions. Several kids report not telling their parents about abuse out of fear. Fear that somehow what happened in my life—with my dad being put on trial for murder—would happen to them and their parents.

After abuse, there are several ways of dealing with the specific situation, and I've spent years counseling and helping others overcome it. Some factors can make the process of healing harder, such as confronting the person who hurt you and dealing with ongoing stress. There are many different ways to heal. There is no one method, no one-size-fits-all approach to healing. You should deal with this type of trauma when you are ready. If you haven't dealt with it, and if you don't feel ready, then wait. If the things you are trying don't work for you, talk to a therapist who specializes in trauma recovery, or find a survivor support group and talk to others to see how they are dealing with it. The important thing is to not give up. There isn't a magic time limit or way to recover. Recovering from any type of trauma will lead you through the entire grieving process. Let yourself feel the emotions that need to be experienced, and allow yourself to grieve. Everyone recovers differently.

There is so much guilt associated with rape and molestation. Young children who had physiological responses of pleasure to any part of what happened to them may experience confusion when family confronts them. Many rape victims find themselves under the microscope of public scrutiny, and they are left wondering if part of their behavior somehow led to someone thinking it was okay to take advantage of them.

It isn't something for which you, as a survivor of any sexual trauma, should ever blame yourself. It was not your fault—never, ever.

CHAPTER 24:

On Grieving

Going through any adversity comes with its own grieving process. Understanding that everything takes time and that you don't have to be okay all at once is important for moving toward becoming okay with who you are and where you are now. Allow yourself to work through each stage. There is nothing wrong with being sad, angry, hurting, confused. You have to let yourself work through those emotions. If you are the friend or loved one of someone journeying through this trauma, give them time and reassurance to feel these things. Don't rush them, and let them talk. It isn't about you or how you feel. Let them process it on their time. Remember, pushing them places them in the mind-set of someone forcing them to do something they don't want to do. Don't be the cause of a fight-or-flight response from someone who is recovering. Just listen.

This complex and profound trauma dwells in the minds and hearts of victims with varying degrees of severity. The survivors of abuse may have endured years of thought programming, distortions of reality, powerlessness. It's imperative to help shift the perspective of the survivor so that they may reclaim their body and realize the power that they do have. The power to heal and to have a successful life.

Moving through the grieving process with a healthy support system in place reduces the risk of an abuse victim remaining in darkness and ultimately reaching the point of utter despair. A victim may experience symptoms of PTSD and have recurring night terrors and daytime memories that can be haunting and even debilitating. Suicide and childhood sexual trauma are heartbreakingly connected at the seams if hope becomes lost. Statistics show that approximately 33 percent of rape victims have suicidal thoughts, and 13 percent of rape victims will attempt suicide. If you or your loved one is having thoughts of self-harm or suicide, please reach out to the National Suicide Prevention Hotline (1-800-273-8255) and get help.

What can you do if you know someone who is going through this grieving process right now? Be there for them. Listen. Speak life and hopefulness into negative feelings that may bubble up for them at times. Remind them that they may fluctuate between the stages of grieving and that they haven't taken a step back in life. Instead, they are healing, and sometimes healing doesn't occur in the same structured order as it may for everyone else. It's okay to grieve the loss of the friend that they thought they had in their abuser. Probably one of the most important things is to be nonjudgmental of anything they tell you in sadness or in anger. All the words, the tears, the good memories along with the bad ones—let it bleed out so the wounds can heal. And like a waterfall, hope will begin to cascade back into that space where pain once dwelled.

This is why I'm here. To tell you that hope is attainable and within reach to every victim. It does and will get better.

I feel that we must have some dreams to give us hope at night before we go to bed. Something to comfort us, something pleasant to think about. I have a few dreams, but I like to consider them goals instead of dreams. I also understand the difference between reality and fantasy, so there's no need to worry. A lot of times I seem like I live in my own little world. That is because we all do. Things are only as good or as bad as our minds make them out to be. I don't know about you, but my little world is a lot happier than the real world. In my world, everyone has hope.

CHAPTER 25:

Back to Normal

After my dad's sentencing, things had already seemed to get back to normal. My parents were back together, and I was back playing football, basketball, and baseball. It was almost like this evil man had never entered our lives. There were a few reminders such as Daddy doing his community service at the Saint George Catholic Church and School right up the road from where we lived. Sometimes I would go with him while he was in a classroom working on a light fixture or some other job. I was back spending time with him . . . and the Catholic school had the same Louisiana history book as we did at Kenilworth Middle School, where I attended. I am not going to confess to getting answers out of the teacher's guide textbook. but let's just say my knowledge of Louisiana history is not what it should be.

I went on to Woodlawn High School, where I played football, basketball, and baseball. My senior year, I also ran track. I lettered three years in basketball. I was a two-time all-district second baseman and a two-time all-district quarterback. My senior year, I was the offensive MVP of the district in football. I was nominated by the *State Times Morning Advocate* as one of the top five finalists for Athlete of the Year in East Baton Rouge Parish.

My fellow Woodlawn High and Kenilworth Middle classmate Danielle Scott took home the honors that night, becoming the first female to win the award. At first, I was disappointed I did not win. But Danielle made me feel better about it by representing the USA in five Olympic games in women's volleyball (1996, 2000, 2004, 2008, 2012) and winning two silver medals, first in Beijing in 2008 and once again in 2012 in London.

In high school, once again, my name was in the paper all the time. But this time for good things. My senior year I was awarded Player of the Week by WBRZ, Channel 2, for my performance against the undefeated and fourth-ranked football team in the state, as well as district challenger, Broadmoor High. I had ten carries for 156 yards rushing with four touchdowns, and I also completed six of seven passes for another 46 yards. I remember when the WBRZ sports anchor asked me to say a few words. I thought, "Do they realize I am the same kid who was kidnapped and whose father shot the kidnapper in the airport?"

I graduated high school in 1990 and was off to college. In 1992, I moved away from Baton Rouge to go stay with my Uncle Jeff in Irving, Texas, in the Valley Ranch area. We lived right across the street from the Cowboys training facility. I wanted to play baseball for North Lake College, but that did not work out. I attended North Lake for two years. I had a wonderful time and made great friends. In 1993, I decided to write this book. I began working on it in my spare time at the North Lake computer lab.

The one cool thing about living in Valley Ranch was going to the Cowboy Sports Café. In 1992 and 1993, the Dallas Cowboys won the Super Bowl, and many of the players hung out at the Cowboys Sports Café. I saw Charles Haley there the day he came to town from San

Francisco. As a matter of fact, Charles Haley bought me my first shot of Goldschläger.

Emmitt Smith, Michael Irvin, and Darren Woodson—as well as lesser-known Cowboy players such as Joey Mickey and Lincoln Coleman—were regulars. On Thursday nights, they would do karaoke. Tony Dorsett was an owner, and we sang together. It was awesome. So for me to get away from home for the first time, that was a hell of experience. I knew about the "White House" back then. The White House was a house close to the practice facility in Valley Ranch where the players would bring their groupies so they were not seen checking into hotels with women who were not their wives. When Jerry Jones approached Michael Irvin about the White House, Michael Irvin said, "I was trying to do the wrong thing the right way."

It was funny because I never appreciated the song "Dirty Diana" by Michael Jackson until I lived in Valley Ranch. The Cowboy Café would be empty except for a few locals, and Emmitt Smith would come in by himself and sit in the corner out of sight, and within ten minutes the place would be packed with twenty stunning, beautiful women. This was before the internet, Twitter, Facebook, Snapchat, etc. How those women knew, I have no idea. My best guess is the waitress had their numbers and would call them.

In 1994, I decided to move back to Baton Rouge to finish writing this book. It never got done.

I reenrolled at LSU and pursued my degree. I always felt I would be a college graduate. I pursued a psychology degree, but the foreign language requirement hindered that plan. I changed my major to general studies, which is basically three minors. I got minors in psychology, philosophy, and speech communications. I want to have lived it and have learned it, and I wanted to give back.

As fate would have it, I was at the student recreation center in 1995 when I read in an article in the *Daily Reveille*, LSU's student newspaper, that Gerry DiNardo, LSU's head football coach, would be the featured speaker at the kickoff for Men Against Violence, a new student organization.

A quick story about Coach DiNardo. In 2017, I was in Sandestin, Florida, on a golf trip with my best friend Randy Leindecker and a few high school football coaches, including two who had been my coaches in high school. I was there to cook. On my way to the store, I was riding in an LSU golf cart, and who comes jogging by but Coach Gerry DiNardo. When I got home, just to be sure it was him, I took a picture of the golf cart and tweeted it to him, asking, "Was that you I saw jogging today in Sandestin?"

He responded back and confirmed it was him. When the fellows got back from playing golf, I told them I had seen Coach DiNardo. Coach Moock, my high school football coach, had met with Coach DiNardo during his tenure at LSU, so he said to tell him hey. What I ended up doing was inviting Coach DiNardo over for dinner the next evening. He showed up with two bottles of wine, ate dinner, and hung out, telling stories for three hours. We had a wonderful time.

Men Against Violence was an attempt to get men involved in the prevention of violence against women, including sexual and physical assault. I wanted to be part of this group. Luckily, my friend David Hagstad was on the board for Men Against Violence. He then took me to a meeting, and I was hooked. I became chairman of support, and I was able to represent LSU at the American College Health Association Conference in Orlando in June of 1996.

Men Against Violence was thought up by our advisor, Luoluo Hong. Luoluo had earned her PhD at LSU. She identified student leaders and was able to get them involved.

The first president was Gabe Northern, a two-time all-SEC defensive end on the LSU football team. Once he graduated and got drafted by the Buffalo Bills, Gabe was still active in MAV by donating money to the group. Years later, in West Monroe, Louisiana, I was having a beer with Gabe at Hooters, watching the NFL draft. Gabe told me, "I am so glad I was part of Men Against Violence. Because there are a lot of people I would like to fuck up, but I'm not."

After graduating LSU in 1997, I wanted to do two things: move back to Irving, Texas, and continue my work in violence prevention. So two weeks later, I headed back to Texas. I stayed with my best friend Dave and his wife for a month before I got my own place. I finally had a place of my own. I needed a job while I looked for work, so I got a job working as a DJ/karaoke host. It didn't do much for my sanity or my checkbook, but it worked wonders on my sex life. There is something about being the star of the show that makes you more attractive to those being entertained.

I did this for a while, and I could not find a job. So I made one of the best decisions of my life. I dialed up the internet, went to CareerPath.com, and checked ten cities (San Diego, Chicago, Los Angeles, New York, Philadelphia, etc.), and I entered the keywords *child sexual-abuse prevention.* What came next was the perfect job description. It was located just outside of Philadelphia—the Victim Services Center of Montgomery County Inc. in Norristown, Pennsylvania.

I had never heard of Norristown, Pennsylvania, and I had only included Philadelphia in my search because I was a fan of the Eagles coach Ray Rhodes. This was shortly after he had been criticized for using a "rape and sodomy" analogy regarding back-to-back Eagles home losses.

I stayed up all night trying to write the perfect cover letter. The next day, I sent in my resume. I received a call from Stephanie Galindo, supervisor of education at the Victim Services Center. She was going to be attending a conference in New Orleans in a few weeks and asked if that would be a place we could do the interview. I jumped at the idea—my niece had just been born, and I was looking for an excuse to go home.

The night before the interview, I stayed with my friend John Delgado, who was in law school at Tulane. He would later become a councilman in Baton Rouge.

I decided to show up to the interview with a copy of an article about the shooting and kidnapping to let Stephanie know why I was interested in pursuing this type of work. During the interview, I let her read it.

Good thing I let her read it because when she got back to her meeting, Judy Benitez, the executive director for the Louisiana Foundation Against Sexual Assault, asked Stephanie where she had been and why she had missed the morning meeting. Stephanie said she'd had a job interview with someone interested in working at the Victim Services Center in Pennsylvania. Stephanie then said, "He is from Louisiana. You may have heard of him. His name is Jody Plauché."

Judy looked at Stephanie and asked, "*The* Jody Plauché?"

Stephanie said, "Yes." So even though I was living in Texas and interviewing for a job in Pennsylvania, fourteen years after the shooting, people still remembered my name.

A similar thing happened in the spring of 2017. I took a trip to New York City, and I found out my favorite comedian, Jim Norton, was going to be trying out new material at the Fat Black Pussycat in Greenwich Village. The cost was only five dollars with a two-drink minimum (which was not a problem). I had first become aware of Jim Norton when a caller had called in to *The Opie and Anthony Show* and mentioned the shooting while discussing the Jerry Sandusky case. Although Opie and Anthony were very popular in Philly when I lived there, I never listened to them.

Over the years, starting in 2012, I have seen Jim perform in Addison, Texas; Dallas, Texas; and New Orleans. After his Dallas show, I introduced myself and let him know my dad was the guy who had shot my kidnapper. Every now and then, I would send him an email, and on this trip in 2017, I let him know I would be in New York City and suggested that if he had a chance, maybe we could grab a bite to eat. So when I got to the Fat Black Pussycat, it was not a surprise when I said hey to Jim before the show. He asked me if I had lost some weight . . . which I had.

I attended the show located in a small room inside the bar. My friend Tiffany joined me as we sat second row, right in front of the stage. Tiffany and I had enjoyed a few cocktails at a bar next door called Off the Wagon before the show and continued sipping libations as Jim tried out his new material. Near the end of the show, Jim looked at this couple and asked the guy what his favorite genre of porn was. The guy sat quietly because he appeared to be sitting next to his wife or significant other. So Jim looked at the crowd and said, "What's your favorite genre of porn?"

Immediately, Tiffany yelled out, "Anal!"

Jim stopped, looked at her, and asked, "Ma'am, do you know who you are sitting next to? That's my friend Jody, and when Jody was younger . . ." He stopped and asked me if it was okay if he shared my story with the audience. I was fine. He proceeded to tell the crowd about the sexual abuse, the shooting, and Daddy not getting any jail time. The crowd applauded.

Tiffany immediately started to apologize. "I'm so sorry. I don't know what I was thinking. I forgot."

I told her, "Don't worry about it. My favorite comedian just introduced me to a crowd in New York City." Moments like that make me appreciate my life and my experiences. And if you are unfamiliar with Jim

Norton, go check out his specials on YouTube and Netflix, or if he comes to your town, go see him live. To me he is up there with Richard Pryor and George Carlin because like those two greats, his comedy is based on his truth and his realities. I look forward to seeing him again, hopefully on the *Jim Norton & Sam Roberts* show on SiriusXM Radio Faction Talk to promote this book.

CHAPTER 26:

Off to Philly

I eventually got the job in Pennsylvania, yet I knew nothing about the town Philadelphia or, more specifically, Norristown. I logged onto AOL to search out people from Norristown, and I would ask them questions such as, "Where is a good place to live?" I was told "Blue Bell, Pennsylvania" and to "stay off Cherry Street." Eventually, my agency-assigned parking spot would be located off Cherry Street for several years. Without incident.

Before I was set to move, I booked a round-trip ticket from DFW to PHL. Got me a room at the Motel 6 in King of Prussia and went and scouted the area for a nice place to live not far from Norristown. As soon as I checked in at the Motel 6, I asked the young lady at the front desk if there was anything to do around the hotel. She said, "I don't know; I'm from Philly."

Me being from the South, I thought, "This is still Philly." King of Prussia is a suburb of Philadelphia, so I thought she should know.

She then said, "Dey got a Hootas up da street." I decided to go have dinner at the old Hooters of King of Prussia off Highway 202. My waitress was Jennifer. I told her how I was going to be moving up there in three weeks, and I picked her brain about the area and how she liked it. We talked for a good while. When her shift was over, she told me she was meeting friends at Uno and suggested I should stop by.

I took the rental car back to my motel room, which was directly across the street from Uno, and met her over there. That is the reason why my best friend from Pennsylvania was a GM at Hooters, my ex-roommate was a cook at Hooters, and 90 percent of my Facebook friends from Pennsylvania either worked at Hooters, managed at Hooters, or were regulars at Hooters. It was the first place I went when I moved up. It was where I would go when I got off work. I didn't know anybody, and I was trying to meet people. One of the cooks and my good friend, Mike McCarthy, whom I barely knew at the time, would make fun of me. He would say, "Hey, Jody, what is that, your third beer, and you have been here for four hours?"

My time in Pennsylvania was great. I got a second job at Lone Star Steakhouse in King of Prussia. I remember one day at work I mentioned I had been on *The Oprah Winfrey Show* and *Traces of Death II*, and I told my story to the few people who were working. My coworker Adrienne called me Pinocchio because she said I was lying. Nobody believed me. I drove back to my apartment, grabbed a tape of me on TV, and headed back to Lone Star to show them I was telling the truth.

When I got back, nobody wanted to see the tape. They told me they now believed me.

"What happened?" I asked.

They told me Monica the bartender—who was an avid fan of A&E shows such as *American Justice*, *City Confidential*, and *Forensic Files*—knew the story and confirmed for me.

Ultimately, after seven years serving the wonderful community of Montgomery County, after receiving the award for Survivor/Activist of the Year, and after Daddy had a serious stroke, it was time to come back home.

CHAPTER 27:

The End

In July of 2005, I returned home. Daddy's health was deteriorating, and he was drinking a lot, eating sweets, and just generally not taking care of himself. He was living alone, and I felt that moving home was the right thing to do. I had gained the experience I'd wanted at the Victim Services Center, and I felt it was time to move on. I had only been back almost two months when Hurricane Katrina hit Louisiana and Mississippi. We were okay in Baton Rouge; we just lost power for five days. But it was my mother I was worried about. She had been living just off the beach in Biloxi for the last fifteen years after leaving my dad, again, for drinking too much.

We got word the next day that her apartment had been destroyed. Completely gone. Good thing she and a few friends had decided to leave town and head to Florida to get away from the storm. Who goes to Florida to get away from a hurricane? But it worked.

I had a few speaking engagements scheduled. A week after Katrina, I spoke in Pittsburgh on a panel at the National Sexual Assault Conference. On the panel was Patricia Bowmen. You might remember her from the William Kennedy Smith trial? We would present again on a panel in Slippery Rock, Pennsylvania, a few months later. Patricia, another panelist, and I stayed at a bed-and-breakfast after the presentation. It was an interesting night. It was awesome to talk to one of the victims of one of the most well-known rape cases of all time.

Being back home with Daddy was not bad. But it did present a few challenges. I came home one night around ten o'clock at night to find Daddy curled up in the fetal position on the kitchen floor. I was not sure if he was dead or alive or just passed out drunk, or maybe he'd had another stroke. I saw his stomach moving up and down, so I knew he was alive. I tried to wake him, but that wasn't going to happen. He was shit faced.

I remember getting pissed off and trying to guide him into the back bedroom. At one point I had to avoid the dog, or a dog toy, and I had to yank him over it. As soon as I did that, I heard a faint, drunken whimper say, "You strong, Jody." I managed to get him to his bed, and I just laid him down.

A few months after that incident, January 2006, I get a call from my mother to go check on Daddy. My brother lived across the street from Daddy, so I told her to call him. She said something was wrong and that I needed to get home now. When I got there, Bubba, Mikey, and Sissy were already there. He had been throwing up blood all day and needed to go to the hospital. The four of us and my brother-in-law rushed him to the hospital.

Once we got to the emergency room, they had to get him a barf bucket. Unfortunately for Sissy and Bubba, they somehow got stuck back there and had to witness it. Mikey and I decided right then and there that they were better kids than us. It really was horrible.

The doctor came in with a checklist of ailments, and Daddy had experienced pretty much every one at some point in his life. When he got to the bottom, he asked if Daddy ever had esophageal varices. I said, "I am guessing this is what he has."

According to MayoClinic.com, esophageal varices are abnormal, enlarged veins in the esophagus, which connects the throat and stomach (esophagus). This condition occurs most often in people with serious liver disease. Esophageal varices develop when normal blood flow to the liver is blocked by a clot or scar tissue in the liver. To go around the blockages, blood flows into smaller blood vessels that aren't designed to carry large volumes of blood. The vessels can leak blood or even rupture, causing life-threatening bleeding.

I was right. They rushed Daddy into surgery to put rubber bands around the bleeding vessels. We were told the prognosis was not good. Mikey, one of my cousins, and I went downstairs to give blood since Daddy was bleeding out. Once we got down there, a nurse put the needle in my arm, and while I was sitting there, looking at Mikey and my cousin, I asked, "What the hell? I thought y'all were giving blood."

My cousin said, "I can't; I'm anemic."

Mikey said, "I can't. I did steroids in high school."

I said, "How is the guy that got fucked in the ass as a child the only one able to give blood?"

The next morning, I got word that the surgery was not successful, and I was told I needed to get to the hospital as soon as possible. A priest was administering Daddy his last rights at that exact moment. I got in the car and headed to Our Lady of the Lake Hospital. When I got to the ICU, the nurses pointed me into the room where Daddy was dying.

I opened the door, expecting the worst, and who was sitting up, attentive, watching TV, and eating ice cream like nothing was wrong? My father. Once again beating the odds of death. If you know that joke about the cat being on the roof—well, Daddy was on the roof for years. Daddy had beat the odds. Because he was on blood thinners from the stroke, he was bleeding out. They couldn't give him a clotting agent to stop the bleeding because then he would have had another stroke. The surgery ultimately worked, and he was as healthy as he had been in a long time.

That day of him throwing up blood and going to the emergency room really scared the shit out of him. He quit drinking (again) and started to try and take care of himself better. He would set doctor's appointments and make them. He was way better now than before I'd moved home. But he was still not in undamaged shape. We knew that he had a blood clot in his brain that could release at any time and kill him.

By September 2011, Daddy's health was in decline. He wasn't as mentally sharp as he had once been; the strokes and ministrokes were taking their toll. One night, he tried to bake a cinnamon roll in the oven with a plastic Strawberry Shortcake plate. Then he wanted me to bring him to the store because he wanted to make a pork-chop jambalaya for the LSU vs. Oregon football game. I was scheduled to cater a birthday party with Mikey. My mother, who had moved back home after Katrina, was going to be in Biloxi. There was no reason for a pork-chop jambalaya.

Before I left to cater the party, I took the knobs off the oven and stove top so he could not use them—so he would not burn down the house. When we got home, he was underneath the carport with a low-pressure burner and a propane tank, cooking his pork-chop jambalaya. I should have left the knobs on the stove; this was much more dangerous.

I remember when it was done, Daddy kept telling me to try his pork-chop jambalaya. "It's good," he said. The next evening was a Sunday night, and my sister was over visiting with my mother when Daddy came walking down the hall, words slurring, leg dragging, and face drooping.

He'd had a much more severe stroke than he ever had before. We rushed him to the hospital once again. This time, he was not coming home. The most unfortunate thing about this was that Daddy's pork-chop jambalaya was excellent. But since he had the stroke the day after cooking it, he did not have the ability to communicate how he'd cooked it. So to this day, I have never had pork-chop jambalaya again.

After he was stabilized, he was not able to take care of himself and required twenty-four-hour care, so we made the decision to place him in a nursing home. Though it was hard for him to communicate and his short-term memory was bad, he still had a personality and a good long-term memory. There were a few incidents during his stay at the nursing home. Once, he tried to leave. He wanted out and walked, slowly, out of the front door. Another time he went "strolling." Strolling in a nursing home is exactly like streaking, except you cannot go as fast. But the one that really got him in trouble was the morning he played dead. Not the best place to pull that trick.

Sissy would visit him every day and sometimes take him to get a margarita. She would take a fishing pole up there, and the nursing home had a pond where he could go fishing. Every Sunday we would pick him up and bring him home, where my mother would take care of him. Sometimes he would want to go back early because he was enjoying his little life in the nursing home.

On this one occasion, my mother was wiping his ass, cleaning him up, and she looked at him and said, "Do you finally regret all the drinking you did?"

My father, naked from the waist down, looked at her and said, "No."

That was when I told her *she* was the one wiping his ass. I asked her, "Do you regret not getting a divorce?"

One Sunday, I cooked some red beans and rice, and Daddy loved them. He got on the phone with Sissy and said, "En umm ehh ehh enn umm umm." I couldn't understand a word.

He handed me back the phone, and Sissy said, "Daddy told me you cooked the best red beans and rice." She had an incredible ability to understand him in that situation.

Another time he was at the house and wanted a beer. My mother asked me, "Can he have one of your beers?"

I said, "Sure." Daddy took that beer and drank it in about three seconds and indicated he wanted another one. My mother brought him another one, and he chugged that one too. He indicated he would like another one, and she told him, "*No*! I'll get you some tea." She brought him some tea, and I calmly walked over to the freezer, grabbed my vodka, and filled up his cup while he sat there with a smile on his face.

In October of 2014, my best friend Dave decided to come to Baton Rouge to attend the LSU vs. Kentucky football game. We had a great weekend. We went and watched my other best friend Randy Leindecker coach a local high school football game against my high school coach's team. I was scheduled to speak at North Lake College in Irving that Monday, so I was going to ride back to Arlington with Dave and fly home after the speech.

That Sunday, we dropped my truck at the Baton Rouge Metropolitan Airport—yes, that airport. As we left, I looked at him and said, "Who do you want to go see—Uncle Jeff or Daddy?" I recommended Uncle Jeff because he was on the way, and his cancer had returned. Fifteen years earlier, Uncle Jeff had battled cancer, and it was back. Uncle Jeff's spirits were down for obvious reasons, so we made the decision to stop by False River and say hey to Uncle Jeff. I told Dave, "Daddy has been in the nursing home for years; we will go see him next time."

Uncle Jeff was delighted to see Dave. He mentioned to Dave that he was "dying." But other than that, we had a great visit. My cousin Reid was there. He stopped by to see his PaPu (grandfather). It was a beautiful day on a beautiful lake. I was glad Dave got a chance to see Uncle Jeff.

The next day, I met with the student group at North Lake and was ready to give my speech. I remember it being very hot and me sweating a bunch. My good friend Savanna Moreland Kwieran met me at North Lake. She wanted to see the presentation. It went great. The highlight for me was one of the professors who stopped by to hear my presentation—he had been at North Lake when I had attended, and he remembered me. While I had been attending North Lake, I had appeared on the shows *Maury* and *Geraldo*, and I had been featured in the *North Lake Student Newspaper*. Jennifer Silver had done a wonderful job telling my story in the newspaper in 1993, just as Grant Ziegler did reporting on my presentation in 2014.

I was able to save an Uber fare because Savanna dropped me off at the DFW airport. I felt so great and accomplished. After doing a presentation, there is a rush, a high. I was floating on cloud nine. I had just given a speech at the college I had once left home to attend, and I had been well received. Plus, I love Irving, Texas, and it gave me an excuse to be there.

I got home around nine o'clock that night. Sat down to unwind and have a beer, or two, or three, or four . . . just before midnight, I rinsed my mouth out in the kitchen sink. (I dip one dip a night, right before I go to bed.) Above the kitchen sink was a picture of my father's hands taken in the nursing home. There was a caption below that said, "These hands, though wrinkled or weak, have been the tools I have used all my life to reach out, grab, and embrace life." I remember looking at it before going to bed and thinking, "And pull the trigger." I also remembering feeling bad for him because he was such a great man, even with all his flaws. He was kind, generous, and funny. Before the shooting, he had been beloved by everyone who knew him. And he grew to superhero status after. I felt bad because someone who meant so much to so many had come to a pitiful end in a nursing home, wilting down to nothing.

I lay down for no more than ten minutes when I heard a car pull into the driveway. It was Sissy. She opened the door and screamed at the top of her lungs that Daddy was dead. She was hysterical. She woke up my mother. She was dry heaving. She was out of her mind. She and my mother left immediately, heading to the nursing home.

I got up and grabbed a beer. I called Mikey and told him. I don't know why I did that because Daddy would have been just as dead in the morning, but I was not thinking straight. Mikey came over, and we drank a few more beers, talking about the life of our father. I got up the next morning and went to work that day. My mother and sister were going to make the arrangements, and there was no reason for me not to work.

The service was that next Friday. Dave, who had just made the drive from Dallas to Baton Rouge, made the drive once again that Thursday so he could be at Daddy's service. When he got to the house that Thursday night, I was paying tribute to my father. I was shit faced. I stayed up all night, waiting for Dave to get there, and the Icehouse beers were going down smoothly. I got up the next morning and headed for Saint George Church. The same church my father had done community service for was now the place he would be on display for friends to pay their last respects.

I stayed to the back of the church. I did not want to see the body of my dead father. Then I got word that Anthony Marabella was there and was asking where I was. Anthony was my father's lawyer. The gang was all there. Mike Barnett, Anthony Marabella, all my dad's living friends, family, neighbors. I had never seen that many people at a funeral in my life.

I stood behind the coffin, greeting the people there to pay their last respects to my father. Dave stood next to me, doing whatever I asked.

He would get me water, hold my suit jacket, whatever. During the service, Dave and I sat together. At one point, I looked at Dave and said, "Do you realize everyone thinks you are my life partner?" He laughed. He is used to my inappropriate humor, often calling me "the worst best friend of all time."

Then I got the word that the news, WBRZ, Channel 2, was outside and wanted me to give a statement. Father Mike, who married Mikey and has known the family for years, asked if we wanted him to send them away.

I said, "No. I'll talk to them." The funny thing is, Father Mike had known my family for years and would do services at the nursing home, which my father would attend weekly, and yet he had not realized my father was the person who had shot the guy in the airport. He only realized it when Daddy died and the local paper shared an article.

I'm not a huge fan of religious services, especially around death, but one moment of Daddy's service stood out. Upon learning of my father's death, a childhood friend, Tracy Smith, posted a note on Facebook titled "Farewell 'Big' Gary Plauché." It was so nice; we were honored to have him read it at the service.

Farewell "Big" Gary Plauché

We grew up in a little village. An enclave in South Baton Rouge. It was a different time, much different from today. Life was simple . . . life was sweet. We all knew each other; we all liked each other. We shared our lives together. There were the McElroys, Achees, McCrackens, Cagles, Grahams, Kuykendolls, Duplantiers, and of course the Plauchés. They were like our family . . . they were our family. We were living in a young neighborhood bound by common threads and common interests: food, football, fun, and of course the children.

We lived in a time before technology . . . we played all day until the sun went down or until we heard Mrs. June yelling, "Jody! Gary! Get home." (We didn't have cell phones; all they had to do was yell down the street, and we would come.) We played Pee Wee Football and CYO Basketball, and we did Y-Indian Guides, jumped on trampolines, built treehouses, played backyard football, caught snakes and turtles, brought home strays, collected cats, dogs, ducks . . . we swam all day at the neighborhood pool. We climbed to the tops of trees. We would set up ramps and jump them with our bikes like little daredevils (we would actually set trash cans on fire and jump them with our bikes like Evel Knievel), much to our parents' dismay . . . but we were fearless. We went on adventures. We would play in the woods back then when there were woods. We would walk down to the Village Grocery, and we would spend all our money on gum and candy. We would see how much gum we could actually fit in our mouths. (My favorite was green apple.) Mrs. June wouldn't allow me in the house. For some reason June never liked green-apple gum. We had cookouts, barbecues, and crawfish boils, and our parents drank . . . lots of beer. On Christmas morning we'd meet out on the streets to play with our new toys: big wheels, Green Machines, Stretch Armstrong, our new bikes, our Evel Knievel bikes . . . and then we would play some more.

We experienced trauma and tragedy together. We slammed our hands in car doors, we broke bones, and we got stiches. We witnessed the drama of life unfold: father and son quarrels, little Gary's (Bubba's) accident at the pool, and when the unthinkable happened, we all stuck together. Mr. Gary stood his ground. And we stood by him. The whole community stood by him. We had a loving fondness for each other. And we looked out for each other. Our dads were from a different generation. They drank to excess, they told jokes and laughed until they cried, and they were men of their word and friend to many.

They were good men. They would scream, and they would yell, but when the moment was right, the tears would flow down their wrinkled faces, and you knew that there was a deep, abiding love inside their hearts. They were tough and tender. They were honest, loyal, and kind. They were our dads, doing the best they could, and despite all their faults, the depth of the love they had for their families was undeniable and unshakable. But Mr. Gary was a dad among dads. He was a sweet-hearted man. I'm not sure if he knew he was great. He was humble, and my guess is that he did not know it . . . but he was. He loved so deeply . . . his wife/the love of his life . . . June. His children: Gary, Jody, Sissy, Mikey . . . and the grandkids.

We are lucky . . . and we are grateful . . . for the life you gave us.

Mr. Gary Plauché was not just a good man; he was a great man. And he will be missed tremendously.

After that it was back to the Catholic Mass.

I made it through, and it was time for us pallbearers to pick the coffin up and place it into the hearse. I walked up to the casket as we were receiving instructions about how to fold the flag and what else to do. I had been strong. I had not shed one tear during the service. I remember looking at Uncle Jeff, who had undergone a chemotherapy treatment since Dave's and my visit just five days earlier, and he looked terrible. His hair was gone. He had not eaten in days. I was sad for him because my father was his baby brother.

The time came for us to lift the casket and put it in the hearse. One . . . two . . . three . . . lift. As soon as I picked up my father's casket, a voice in the back of my head went off—it was the same, faint, drunken whimper saying, "You strong, Jody." As I lifted my father into the car that would take his body to be cremated, I thought, "We all are. We are a strong family to have gotten through everything we have been through and be this close."

That night, Mikey and I went to the Saenger Theatre in New Orleans to see Alton Brown. The next night, LSU beat Ole Miss. Nothing in the world changed. Except the opposite thing happened when Daddy shot Jeff. When Daddy shot Jeff, the world became a little bit better. When Daddy died, it got a little bit worse.

I want to end this book the way I have ended every speech I have given since 2003. I was doing a presentation in Johnstown, Pennsylvania. The brochure had a quote on it, and I said I would use this quote until the day I die. It was a quote from Helen Keller. It said, "Although the world is full of suffering, it is also full of the overcoming of it."

ABOUT THE AUTHOR

Jody Plauché has worked in the field of violence prevention since 1995.

While attending Louisiana State University, he served on the executive board for Men Against Violence, a campus organization aimed at preventing campus violence, including sexual assault and physical violence.

After graduating from LSU, Jody worked at the Victim Services Center of Montgomery County, a comprehensive crime-victim center in Norristown, Pennsylvania. At the Victim Services Center, Jody worked as a sexual-assault counselor as well as a prevention educator, and he eventually became the supervisor of community education programs. Jody provided crisis intervention to sexual-assault victims on the agency's twenty-four-hour crisis hotline as well as through in-person support at hospitals and police stations.

Jody facilitated sexual-violence risk-reduction programs for students ranging from pre-K to college. He also presented numerous professional training sessions for police officers, hospital staff, parents, and school administrators.

Jody also served on the statewide Men Against Sexual Violence committee.

In October 2002, he attended the White House Conference on Missing, Exploited, and Runaway Children in Washington, DC, featuring Colin Powell and President George W. Bush.

In 2004, Jody was named the Survivor/Activist of the Year by the Pennsylvania Commission on Crime and Delinquency.

Jody has shared his personal story as well as his knowledge about working with survivors of sexual assault on numerous TV shows, including *Geraldo, Now It Can Be Told, Maury, The Oprah Winfrey Show, Leeza, Real TV, The Montel Williams Show, The John Walsh Show,* CNN's *Connie Chung Tonight, ABC World News Tonight,* and ESPN's *E:60.*

Made in the USA
Monee, IL
29 July 2024